Anatomist
Poet

Ayad Gharbawi

authorHOUSE®

AuthorHouse™ UK Ltd.
500 Avebury Boulevard
Central Milton Keynes, MK9 2BE
www.authorhouse.co.uk
Phone: 08001974150

Published by AuthorHouse 11/14/2012

ISBN: 978-1-4772-4276-6 (e)
ISBN: 978-1-4772-4277-3 (sc)

Table of Contents

A Portrait Of Life – Suicide of a Priest

Killers killing
Lovers loving
All are One
Praying to randomly chosen godless minds
That priest sacrificed himself, did you not hear?
Yes, call it suicide, if you want
In your brilliant mind
Did it matter really?
He was screaming silently
In his numbest depths
No one was remotely interested
The sounds of mental mutilations
Were too explicit to be reasonably viewed
And you know
He was never equipped for all this
That God
Dished out to him, dear Soul
For it was surely such a plate too full for
Such a gentle roving mind as his.

He tried to stand
And escape out
From these
Heated drenching waters
Idiotic smiles seducing his mania
That succeeded in expanding with such ferocious
Malignancy in his brain
Causing him to die in the manner that he did

Eyeless smiles; were they sincere or threatening?
He expected so much from this merry earth
But was instead seeing more and more
A crass dull future
Tell me then, Sir
Of your lurid poetry
What were you trying to say to us?
And do you think it did matter
Or, it didn't matter?
What you ever said
Or what you ever did do
Self murdering priest
Did you destroy any of your listeners
Out for a measure of 'fun'

Exactly as ruling Liars discussing and dictating their 'truths'
On everyone else
Was that your theological world?
Was that the sum value and relevance of your priestly life?

ॐ

A Love That Not Even Jesus Could Live With

Sweetness
My love for you
Was bitter in its essence
It was
All in all
Far too much
For you in its
Absurd Intensities

I guess
I know now
Even sincerest love may wash away
Seeking a breath and an escape from my persisting worries

What you felt for me
Was what?
Was it
A 'Love' that
Not even
His Holiness, Jesus could live with?

And so,
So many,
Out there
Will prefer crucifixions
That are endless
To a quiet and deeply adoring patience
That I had for you.

&&

A Madman's Gesture

In my bedrooms of a time I called yesterday
The evenings were excessively red I felt
The sunsets meant something final to me
A hand of adoration gestured meaningfully
One sentence expressed its intent to kill me
Where else did I paint these scenes of my life?
They were all my own experiences

I witnessed your conversations
The attempts
In instances hopeful to convince me of my bemused folly
I, in my turn, did try once or twice
To create
The hope of love
To fulfil you Strangers out there sitting
Glancing nowhere, yet you preach to me
Walking pointlessly, yet you admonish me
And you are all ultimately colliding against each other

Where do I exist?
I exist in my mind, safe and secure
I can be, I can express every emotion
You ask me repeatedly, "Do you or do you not Love?"
Yet, in loneliness' laws
Who exactly is there
To love?

෨෬

A Sailor's Letter

Monument's finale, as it ruts away
Requiem disguised, for an End has arrived
An act to move through, we must do so
So at last, the
Words crossing the land of shameless criminals
Have come to see Justice being applied
See the laughter of virgin tears being vindicated
Don't you turn away again now, after all that you have done
Can't you see these uncivil sinister trivialities you oppressed us with?
You said unto us, "I'm so alive, I can feel every moment in this life!"
But do not lie to me
No north, no south can now change these disturbed winds
Wither do they vanish, or wither do they rest?
None is relevant
Between us now
This moment defines
Your Existence's expanses have come to their end
What grips your indefinable, unruly senses
Are copies of the same
Immaterial emotional fakery that so did chain us
Your mind, within and your pretending mind outside will be cast unto these waves
And all can see are your acts so feigning, so pretentious
Your bride of cruel visions will now experience the meals you forced us to eat
I see you are still Lying, trying to ignore your disrupted mind
Your infrastructure that was so burdensome to all of us peasant sailors
Is bearing its collapsing crashing weight on you
Between us now
Yearn for this now to end
For the now
Is the definition true
Of existence
The existing now moment
Is what your Self is
Confront your scavenging rootless eyes
Your Loneliness will have its nourishing roots fed
Your thousand detrimental deceptive rainbows that gave us 'Hope'
Will now Mock your remaining sanity
So illusory
Upon their borrowed masks
We will now be effectively employed to
Entertain and torture you
So

Don't take it all so seriously
Words you mentioned did once kill, didn't you understand?
Ah! The symphonic movements of sincerity's passions between us
In the stillest hours of solitude sigh
Have now come to maturity
And yet, within contexts of raging panting thoughts
Inside caged ears
Surely you knew the victory would be Ours, indeed?
So forget your desires, your needs essential now
Remember all others who you tortured
The fiery dead and the numb living who once
Had such interesting arguments on decency and morality
But are they not all soon to be one with you?
Yes, your decayed compass
Turns inside out
Betraying you
You lost your direction, and plunged yourself inside the fiercest storm
That churned your entire memories, the good and the bad, into a mosaic of madness
You either hear or you do not hear
And now you talk about 'Love' and 'God'!
Laugh, friendless bastard, laugh seriously
Now you shall feel the serious reality of your own plays
Sweet human, how much longer did you think you could spin?
Why?
Couldn't you do better?
Couldn't you have been more compassionate?
Couldn't you have been more understanding?
No?
So, be cast away Humanity!
Lie in your fragrant bowels of crimes
Lie to your sickening madness that loves butchering fanatically
Lie!
To your spastic shudders of evil emotions that reverberate within you
Giving you the spasmodic pleasures of intense pain
Ignore the polite, stern winds emerging, demanding truth, justice and peace!
For until
You will Bow your soul, Man,
Until you will bow your sanity to God above you;
Respond respectfully, understandably
And try to think truthfully
No peace of mind will ever Grace you.

◌◌

A Vile 'Human'

An evening
Supper's Traitor sitting gleeful
Begins the eerie epochal moment
To willfully extinguish
A life's fragile candle.
The incomprehensible scenes I see
In my silent eyes
Seemingly never ending
Wild expanses
Visions of Hurt, Sorrow and Loneliness.

Seeking any role to play
We turned for comfort
To the guided Fool
Look at the utter beauty of the liars
Around you
Spelling mistakes
That changed your brief life.

Do not lie about your mistakes
Listen to your deathly end
Coming so soon
Silence and Symphony
For all your moments
To ponder about.

And you are still acting, despised 'human'
Acting beyond reason and its compassion
My God!
I shall soon meet you!

Ancient victim,
Still writing
Your scripts for idiotic lovers
I will tell you
Do not stand for the Remorse of Judas.

Forsaken children,
Abandoned by the vilest creatures Man has known
Tears of a Farewell
Are screaming
An endless Farewell
Ending this human life
And finally so.

೦೯

A Wife's Pleas

Come to please
This life
That so suffers
Her insides
Out:

In my life
That you love
I can only see
What truths
Can be so
Killing me.

৪৫

A Word to My Tormentor

Let me go home
Please
In this night here
Stretched out
For all the lies
I've had to endure
My life has been
A Life of Deprivation
Whilst your life has been
A Life of Depravity
And you force me
To sit here and endure
You

My ears are stolen
My heart is ripped
While your unending words
Are punctuated
By stabbing knives
And by your repulsive
Broken Tongue.

&

Abused Children

You laugh
In your mind
Because they scream
Inside their intricate walls;
Sorrowful children
Who see pain
As their pillow -
I tell you
What an imagination can create
These unstructured and untamed monsters?
Children of orphans,
Crying silently for a penny
Who do you think will be your friend
In these bitter moments?

୭୧

Accepting Yourself

When the evening
Cries out for its disunited heart
To be reasonable
Facing a blurred Truth
Wherein no emotional unity can ever exist
Yes, life is a Trial
From which concrete evidence is unacceptable
For all of you
The needy struggling ones and the unsupported anxious ones;
The dying ones and the flippant laughing ones
No one you love or hate
Wants ever to get to know you
Since you know nothing of yourself
And so, what exactly is there to learn?
And remember that in your own moments of brief ecstatic dawns
And euphoric twilights
Will all come to be forgotten by you
For all the voices and the words you loved to hear
They that whisper to you
Shall forever
Remain enclosed and buried.

You look so surprised!
Didn't you know, dear friendless friend?

☙

Advice of a Sorrowful Woman

Sweet one
I know of you
Where an illness suddenly fatal called 'Love'
Can be within all of us
You know
Aggrieved Hearts can and certainly will wither innocent tongues
For the Liars and the Compassionate ones
United; on and off
I am, I feel, I know
That is Who I am!
I guess
In your room, you lie
And who will be there
Twenty years hence
As the same Mind?
I ask you
As you pen down the drowning words of your life
And your pain
And your grievances
Loneliness; emptiness and other familiar adjectives
I tell you: "Die quietly"
Is it not, all that you may do?
For all rottenness insists on expanding in you
You surely shall stand amidst it all
Only to fall a brief while later
Will you understand then, these my words of counsel?
Will future Children and other Minds understand?
I doubt it, really.
(Laughter)

ᛒᚷ

Advice of an Introvert

Eyes hidden
And laughter
Becoming
Fake
Children of Hurt
And Hatred may be
Within you
Understand the origins
I tell you
In life
In peace
That are frail
All sorrows
Shall begin to be stronger
And souls shall weep
Themselves to dying grief
They question
All your moods
And your wretched work
Defies you
Within
And you shall see
My words
In you
Tell me
Your needs

If you know
Who they really are

Therein lies
Your taunting torments
I tell you

Speak of your needs
And let us Begin therefrom.

ৡৡ

An Analysis of 'Politics'

One Madman to another:
"Your Fame, my Misfortune!"
And the other Madman replied:
"And your Shame, my Glory!"
And people in general
Saw two fierce irreconcilable Hatreds;
In their destructiveness
The two Madmen
Were deemed to be far apart and too unacceptable
For sweet discontented Civilization.
And so, society locked both of them up and away
Leaving them in their
Obsession that was deadlocked
A stalemate of trenches and fruitless Fury.
"Pathetic judgements!"
Judged civilised society, upon the two Madmen
Whose circumstances were becoming rather dire;
"Why did they choose and insist on following
Such savage paths?" asked society innocently.

But, tell me, *you*:
Isn't that
What
Politics is all about?

༒

An Ancient Epitaph

A tramp
Gesticulated coldly
Talked about abstract mathematics
And inquired about love.

An ad was placed
For a dead hero
By a friend who spoke rehearsed jokes
As his destiny turned chaotic
And became momentarily frightened.

Memories sincerely decaying
As the footsteps
Your culture painted
All turned abstract.

&c.

An Awakening

I hear an Awakening!
Hark!
Awaken Ye souls weary!
Awaken!
Aches yearning for fulfilling meanings are coming!
In the passions of stillness
I feel oceans whispering softly
Words of peace that may or may not come so soon;
I feel the hungry ones
Calling out for stale, shreds of fodder
I hear within us all
Harmonies between conflicting souls
Ending in fatalities
Unity of lovers being one!
I hear
Children's tears colouring my black, dry, freezing heart
And I can hear
The sudden sighs of the severely
Mature abandoned children
Can't you yourselves hear yet
This beautiful island of the sorrowful?
Everywhere we are, and yet so isolated
We dither.

⊗⊗

An Old Suicide Note

From my eye
That once
Used to win
And now
Getting to be
Upset
In my own blood
That is still
So unreal
To me.

So goodnight to all
Farewells!
Now I can gossip
About Death
That so far
May happen,
Just happen
Tonight.

❦

Anatomy of What Life Is

Life is tears demanding rights
Life is rage against injured injustices
Life is aggrieving anger at one's wretched lot
Life is gasping painfully
Frustrations against persisting stupidities
Frustrations against deliberate misunderstandings
Confusing different minds, cultures and liberties
Different backgrounds, different languages
Against each other

So listen to your own voices
Record your own voices
And you shall see the degrees of difference
In what you 'are' and what you 'think' you are
And what people 'think' you are
And what History will think of you
In essence we are all alone
In essence we are the Sad
Governments and politicians and jobs and humans mean nothing
Humans kiss and betray and betray and kiss
Can we look beyond our restricted, confined selves?
Can we ever look above the blurred, dazed selves?
Do you perhaps see the shades and shadows of rusty keys and cages?
Wherein we are trapped and entrenched within?
Standing alone
Feeding alone
And fading alone
While no one will feel for you today, nor tomorrow
Gentlemen of this Earth
Yes, in haste I do write
For I do not know
The number of my days
Gentlemen of this Earth, past, present and in the far future
I wish to inform you
What you may or you may not know
I tell you all
You are rapists in earnest
You are molesters and Pharaohs grand
And you may see yourselves for what you are
Or you may not see yourselves
Women of this Earth
I ask you; do not act out the imagination
Of what sick men dream you are supposed to be

Do not be and do not feel emotions
In the image of what
Perverts wish for you to be
Do not ever be the rapists' ambitions
And so thereby feeding his justifications
Around the sweating world, around oppressive jobs and lifestyles,
Around these pointless, fruitless evenings
We were looking forward to
With such pleasured anticipation
Around the bland, tasteless dinners,
Around the murderous years of humble draining boredom
Around the scarred and vague memories I ask you, I question you
Wherever you are, wherever you may exist
The sorrow within you
Your lives, your student days, your jobs, your conversations
Your holidays, your shopping
Your imprisonment, your family, your children
Your coming death, your love affairs
And where do you all lean to
Where do you all gather then?
While you are all busily existing and dying together in your lives
Of an unemancipated painful truth!

∽∾

Are You Going To Be Real With Yourself?

Who is thinking tonight?
On his life and her miseries?
Self inflicted
Please!
Do not ever tell me
It is anything otherwise
For you are
Your greatest
Enemy
I'm far too tired to
Hear, feel anything else
From someone like you
Be your Self and so face your truth
That is your reality
Who lied to whom?
Who deceived whom?
Who stabbed whom?
Do you not know?
How long do you hide from your perverse grins?
How long will you strut around?
With your heard dangling there next to your
Lies and other fabrications from your mind?
You love, you get hurt
Driest story for you humans
You try, you fail

And now
You face yourself
Once again alone
Or that's how I see your Self
Will you face up to your forged Self?

ᘒᘓ

Baby Boy – If Only You Could See Me

If you could see me
A life
Living
In her infancy
Surprising words
Strange yawns
Surrounding me
My baby boy
I am
Losing
Both you and I

I accept death
I surrender
My words
Are meaningless in any case
And in any language
Baby son
I loved you
Desperately

৵৹

Baby Boy

Beloved boy
My only son
My only love
My life
My soul's breath
I talk to you
This pleasant nippy night
Pleasingly Chilly
Tell me
If you can
What words may inspire you
Within you
What?
Darling son of mine
This April night
You sleep
This warm moment
As I look at your grace
I speak
Within myself
From a truth
That has been
Here so much within my
Life

What meanings can succeed to say
To you
That I love you dreadfully so
While I swim in some
Underground London dungeon
Swimming through the hairy rats
But
I always
Feel for you
Your soulful curious eyes
And I scream
These puzzled eyes
That stare right back at me
Izzet!
My beloved angel
Painted by Michelangelo
I bow to you
Serenely

৪৩

Baby Izzet

Sweet son
Listen then to my
Dreams
That have been
So far and away
In lands of awful yonder
And more
Trust my heart
Young one
Trust my only heart
That flaps
For one day
You, too, shall see
These hellish truths that I have been
Through
My young boy
I tell you, Son
The shocked winds will speak of frenzied twists
Within history's painful passions
Brought on
By none else
Except us mortals here
On this sorry land
Of ours
Young boy;
My eternal love
Listen, then, if you can
Listen to my soul's breathing
Palpitating
Izzet
No one else shall care
For you
So much
As I did
Izzet
No one
Can care for
You
As much
As I did.

☙❧

Battered Child's Testimony

A sunshine that sparkled quietly
Rainbows of necessary ambitions that wilt
Oceans of hate collapse in evil
Evil for fun, evil for no reason
Sunshine someone dreamed of
Dreaming from the sorrows of the crooked,
Twisted and repeated years
Where a little girl receives rape as Man's
Reason and desire's needs.

Life anywhere continues
Ancient woman weeping
Modern woman crying
The intervals and gaps mean nothing to me
For the bleeding ones
They march in circles
Circles vague as their lives prescribed.

Irrelevance is a powerful concept today
I exist here today
Soon, I shall be as ancient as the others
While the intelligent people continue
With their words of reasons and smugness
Students in classrooms I have never seen
Pour out their literature on sanity and its values
And are repeatedly taught
The intricate values of zero;
Out there, children on drugs and dull careers
And learning Evil's persistent wisdom.

Trust the none
Hate the all
Survive for the only one
That is you.

And you may feel
And achieve a measure
Of dust's worth
While the storms of the powerful
May stampede upon your heart and love
What you feel, my imaginary friend
Is an act of *irrelevance*
Irrelevance to the globe of toiling people
What you feel, you must forget
What you love, you must abandon.

And, as you shall wilt soon
You too must turn away
And face the death of the Meek
The death of the unknown Christs.

&

Begging Soul

Come to hear
A tearful word
That so begs
An unheard Hatred
To begin to love
In her blackened life;

If only we can
Live
In this trial
Of such a beautiful
Ending.

୫୯

Birth of Sorrow

From my life
I gave in

Surrendering to
A sudden
Realisation

Of such
Serious Sorrow

That so wrecked
My once
Secure life

And therefrom
I did
Suffer.

&

Bitterness

A child wrote Sermons
She hoped would be practical
From experiences harsh
The years of exile troubled the handwriting
And trembling, the child questioned the worth of writing more
For what was termed 'value' or 'worth' was uncertain
I heard a nun violently sing of rape
While professionals in business
Yelled, "Why did you become a recluse?"
The dagger was thrust in a vicious energy of intent
And flesh was slashed and sliced deep
A scream gasped spontaneously
The murderer wanted heroin of the fairest quality
The victim was a loner of no value
So None mourned the victim
None saw the victim so poetically sprawled lifeless
And four days later, I saw a woman beg
For the last speck of food
Begged for the last fragment of garbage
How astonishingly strange,
When the friendless feel so much mature depths
Yet, what can you write of loneliness?
There are no events in Solitude's lifespan
No, loneliness, as such, is but a word
It's up to you to feel it
To feel the sufferings of ordeals
The experiences of hardships
On a daily basis.

৯৫

Can I Breathe?

If I try and dare to breathe
Must it still Cost me so much
When I just
Don't expect to have the money?

෯෯

Blinded Eye

Uncertainties
That faint
In their sudden life
Beginning to create
A passionate being
That suffers
From an embarrassing
Self–hatred
That begs to kill
Her only
Eye's belief.

&

Certified Failure

Good evening to the times so far
My memory has just begun to be realistic
In its persistent fantasies
I begged
In my bizarre life
Trying to untangle the energetic myths
Lying sleepily in between my softly hazy words
I guess I tried too little
Over these years
That have now so passed away
Please understand, then
What a momentary truth may be
Religiously believing in the colourful cause
And then, only to find yourself
Somewhere far away
And lost as a certified Failure

ॐ

Chains Mental

See angels
In your mind
In their paths undefined still
See the mirror
Staring at you
Yes, you
All along
I knew that was my message
I tried to give within you
In the edgy eyes of hatreds
That saw somewhat too much
I tried to explain
In my life limited
By chains mental
Ah! But you ought to have known my
Friendless friend!
Somehow I deemed all others
Somehow more understanding
I guess I misunderstood it all
All in all

જી

Chants of Ancient Wisdom

An angel tried to speak to a
Frail prostitute
Speaking chants of ancient wisdom
But she was
Ignored by the dancing whore
Who loved her lush sins
Far more than she cared for her
Fragmenting sanity

New-born baby boy
I love you
You speak to me
In riddles
And I'm getting older with my mind
So may we ever be serene together?

Polite fake woman
Speechless I stand
As I listen to you
This process is self-destructing
We are tortured
By a blinding numb
Boredom
And the play continues still
So what is this all about?

Beautiful child
Speak to the thousands of years
That now stand before you
And blanket yourself against this biting bitter
Rain

&

Christian Disciple

Silent Martyr!
How can I hear you, then
If all the Tears
You speak of
Burn
My Face
Etching
*Their **Hatreds***
All over
My brain?

છક

Circle of Evil

In this circle we just saw
The experience of a proven
World of scenes
Seen before
Just behind your back
There it rests
While you live
To repeat
The wanderings of another tribe of Prophet Moses
Proving to you
Futility of Man.

This failure
Of a once seething heart
How alive you were!
In my memories
And this night
I hear you are cold
And dead
And so, another page
Must end with the demise of another
Gripping character
From another presumably worthy chapter in our lives

Won't the readers and spectators all tremble with interest?
Or will they fade, and be bored
From all these exploits and deeds and conversations by Man?
There can only be a triumph of evil, I tell you
And for now
There it does flourish
Beneath all their spicy teeth
They will kill once more
Throwing themselves against the little ones
And when, I ask you, will they themselves fade away
To be cold and dead?

୭ଓ

Circus of Life

An eyeless Monk confidently preached of the intricate complexities of the
Visions of Reality that he read somewhere;

The proud and haughty whore wept tears for
The literature she wrote
To illiterate moronic and strangely self-satisfied humans with lots of greedy gold coins;

Another sorrowful dove was harpooned yesterday, I felt
And I did dream of a boy awaiting to be gently impaled
Strange days, while the retarded games of fortune continue
To be churned out by the venerable
Institution of the Television industry
Confusing all well wishers beyond politeness and exasperation
Still, someone shouts:
"Who can decide when the games shall cease?"

So, anticipation is in the murky, deathly air
As you wait to see her death, while she anxiously awaits her final exit;
Some hour later, they raise her to the questioning skies,
All watch in predictable belief and horror unheard of
Downwards she is released, flying fiercely towards a box filled
Yet, we never knew what it was filled with, so strange to relate;
She bounced from the huge box back into the air saddened
Till sweet, merciful death overtakes her
And all announcers analyze peacefully that all is at an end.

You know, I wondered what her crime was
To be worthy of such a tortuous death?
And this earth of yours somehow revolved still without excessively
Being repulsed by what happened
Tell the teenagers their pregnancies are burdens they cannot yet grasp

Those dying on the avenues of glamour and wealth
You have all wasted your minds and lives;
And the politician painted himself with silly images and visions
Both schizophrenic and empty
And insisted on speaking to yawning masses.

And still
There are humans who are faintly surprised
At our earthly life
That is decaying our stench infested souls
Do not ignore the Sad of the Earth

Do not ignore the Punished of the Earth

I warmly tell you.

෨෨

Coming of Death

Kill a meaning from the truth
Whistles of whispers
Where she just looked from her corner
An eye of disbelief
Crumpled rejections forsaking them
Darkened gardens
'Neath black heavens
And her violet crimson dress
Black haired beauty
You have loved here just too late
Sweet angel
The ancient letters were inscribed
By elderly souls just trying to
Explain
Out there to you
And to everyone else, really
So, tremble now
As God awaits you
And you Him.

Evening of triumphs
Raise your arms
The hatreds to wipe out
Arrives
From a reddened crucifix
They dared to stare at us
You wrote your letters
From a beautiful heart
Beaten by ageless evil
Called relatives and friends and lovers
And now, Heaven lands upon us
Upon my mind and yours
We've been waiting in ignorance
For far too long
We can no longer laugh at others
For that kind of laughter inspired the devils to teach even more
Teaching the fiends' tricks of ultra deception called 'love'
Gentle girl
Alone in your brain
Heaven now echoes your aches
We're all blinded
Just till the remaining moments left for us on earth
Till we get there
This human dust of evil is receding from us
And our needs for the widest oceans
Are so near to our lips.

☙❧

Confessions of a Professional Idiot – [Myself]

I have repeated myself
A million times
Imagine
Explaining my squalid behaviour
And humans did understand me
And, of course
I never realized
That everyone,
Yes, everyone
Understood my Self;
But, I myself never did
Understand my own Self
Throughout my existence
And
That, in itself, was
Yet another
Unbelievably
Idiotic
Grand Folly of mine;
And, of course,
Not surprisingly,
I never did even 'understand'
That truth

&&

Confused Woman

Speak your tongue
And say words of your needs
To echo in these corridors of your Self
Within the chambers of your Soul's Heart

Tell me, then
Of your eye's woes
Their frantic, confused expressions
That paint History's supposed meanings

Why did your Essence forsake you?
Do you know?
Stranded there, you are, compassionate Beauty
And so, you fail; didn't you know?

Yes! Look, seek, and knock
In your wisdom's Mirror;
You did try to understand these unformulated, uncoordinated passions
Expressing Truths within your Self -
And, yes, always
They leave you lost ever more;
Do you now understand why
Compassionate Beauty?

෨෬

Confused Madman Begging

I'm not clear
Here about my life
But Christ
I fear myself
From myself
And if anyone could understand me
Here
I guess
I'll hope they'll have a Cure
Serious

So please be with me
Here
Just as I did try to be
With your Self and Soul
It did hurt
Please
Understand
Little outside my pain
Allowed me
To feel or think
For anything else

&c&

Contradictions in Life

A love
Ends
And a truth
Suspended
No longer
Finally
Begins to
Laugh
At herself.

Unbelieving eyes
Come to feel
Here
This now **moment**
That has so
Despised
Your only lifetimes
Achievements
Of worthlessness.

❦

Conversations Betweeb a Sane Man and an Insane Woman

In every day
I see her speaking her mind
She is
Not aware
Really
I tell you
Because
She never is
In being with herself
With her Soul
I think she is Mad
Sitting
As she does
All her hours

In Black and Blue
Anyone pays for her
I guess
She is suffering
And still, somehow
She lives on
And whenever her Mind opens
She gets cursed
By herself
And I get to no longer care
For her or for anyone else
Nothing much matters to me
So maybe I lie to you too
Because I think
Truths are irreconcilable.

Woman of a truth
Anywhere in a town
A village
I see you again
If you speak to me today
Why is your heart veiled
By hour hurt
You know, you must Scream
Your truths
In your Heart of Hurt
Yes, I do know the lies penetrating
I realize the fetid souls you've been influenced by

Woman of truth
We're not even true to ourselves
Let us, try, to realize that, can we?
These are our days
The miserable ones
So why do you and I persist
Fearing our fear
Fearing our own Self
Scared from our Vulnerability
Scared of our Ugliness
But Woman, I tell you
There is no ugliness
There is no need for your fear
It is but a creation of your past memories
Can you actually understand my words?
My feelings?

"And now I speak
"This Lady you say is Mad!
"An evening that may be bright with Hope
"Breathes and hovers over stained luxurious carpets
"From antique wines and tattered garments
"And raped perfumes
"Where Lovers are being
"In love
"Or they are speaking fast
"Across mindless avenues
"Of cities of Death
"Begotten by refugees born from other tragedies
"Can you hear me, ye Souls?
"Ye angry Souls?
"In your pleasant circumstances wherein resides stinging shame
"Winds of manic hatreds
"Sweeping the children
"Children of pained childhoods
"Children begotten by demanding viciousness
"Where colossal mountains weep
"All you listeners! All you Hearers!
"Can you open your Degraded hearts
"Because there is a growing Pain
"Screaming its Truth
"And yet Death is its attached Twin
"How much you understand?
"How much do you wish to sacrifice for Truth, pitiful Man?
"How much you actually Do and Act?

"Souls of Hurt!
"Come and gather near me;
"For we all stand tired
"The Sane and the Insane
"For, I tell you, no one understands us anyway!
"So what difference does it make
"If we were Sane or Not?
"Nobody will ever call us 'Family'
"And, in fact, no one is here
"We're all alone here
"Didn't you know?"

❧

Croation Waitress

Beauty lass
Croatian sweetness
In sudden poverty
And fear;
Lost child
In a London town
Of so much
Alienation –
Could you then
Relate?
Sweet statue waitress
Coming to live
In your empty pockets
That so
Pull on
Your morality.

ൟ

Cynical Bible

An anger of a faceless image crossed my vague path
As a humble meek and dry soul
Rotted in distances absurd
We stood aghast numbed
The deathly hating twists of existence's laughter that attacked us
For no reasons save hatreds' needs
To curse I saved myself, my composure
Till wars and insane choirs overtook mania quiet and unmentioned
The challenges that erupted exotically
What question did your lover ask you tonight?

What thoughts did you remember tonight?
What smiles did you try to fabricate in your innocence

That denies the truths wide and empty?

Yesterday's memories reminded me of myself as a fluid chance and of a particular mask

I couldn't remember
What monks sang in their vows of stupidity, I cared not

What eloquences by politicians praising themselves, I felt not

What immoral, repulsive parents preached, I heard not

What sleazy, thieving religious humans counselled, I felt not

What the advanced, genius textbooks spoke of, I heard not

What sick, dysfunctional society warned me, I listened not

What two faced, hurting, stabbing friends admonished me, I heard not

Meanwhile as the throngs of criminals disguised as men of religion
Themselves misunderstood their roles to play out on us all
While artists, elites and intellectuals danced joyously naked with their shrivelled ideals
And committed crimes unspeakable, beyond the pale
The Immaculate Young Lass died yesterday
Another will die tomorrow
What essences and meanings could I achieve in that time context and frame?
All will fade
All will betray
All will die
As the Saints may speak in me and in you
Of their harmonies and prayers
Well, I heard nothing
Nothing of truth
Nothing of relevance was for me
Nothing of meaning for my self
Nothing of my existence existed
Everything else died within myself
Alongside the Immaculate Young Lass

Ꙭ

Cynicist Finally Speaks

I heard an evasive answer where I was giving an unreal answer
An answer forgotten in its midst
Where my Saintly Errors vanished
Vanished from the brotherhood of my eyes
My eyes that withered in their vision irregular and of chance
Woman that I saw years and moments ago
Tell me your sensitivities that have excited you
Your ships that have sailed erroneously in winds unfortunate and unpleasing
Good, my godless heavens
Why are we going to converse tonight?

That is my question

For my laughter cynical

For my laughter hating

Don't ignore the understanding achieved by two proud drunks
Believe in all directions of scheming, dubious reality
Whistle quietly
As truths travel sluggishly
You'll appreciate
And don't cry your personal tears for whatever reason
Your conversations go on for no reason
Equally random is love
Friendships are accidental and truly temporary
Just as alliances are beneficial mutually
Don't laugh seriously, don't cry
Exist, friend, just hold tight
And be
Wherever you are
And whenever

&❡&

Death is Freedom

Don't tell me
We all don't die
Understand my words
And then
We can live
Fulfilled in our punished minds
Can you tell me here
Where else we can go?
As this life is but a trial run by friendly psychopaths
And we can love it too
For a little while, anyway

Before you and I sleep here
For this last time
Our eyes united in a quiet sleep
Far, far from this time of ours
And our dreams soon turn to truth
Within which
We then live in
Forever more!

૭૯

Death of a Candle

The Candles' eye
That tries to express
Her passions' needs
While you all scream
Threatening to wilfully
Murder her

Beautiful Candle!
Trying not to
Flicker
Into an eternal extinction

I ask you all
Now
People of this life
How Hard can you
All become?

Warm essences and vehement smiles
Facing human steel
Co-imagining somehow
In between this confused air
Breathing and escaping

Angel Candle
Why humans seek your extinction
I do not understand
For what crime have you done
Save to enlighten men, women and children?

Your life
I tell you
Is ending.

⸭

Death of a Confident Man

And are
People still trying to preach
Sermons of
Words deeply philosophical
To you?
Didn't you guess?
They were aiming for you;
And you sat confidently there
Throughout this
Your life
That you did betray
By the way
Didn't you guess
What you did against your own flesh
And mind?
The scaffolds of your execution
Stare at you
They wish to be seen with
Your final seconds
Your efforts have gone dead
You're losing this game
Foolish friend
You're losing
This game that
You once
Thought yourself
To be oh so
Conquerable

&c.

Death of a Friend

Say to us
Hurtful Words
Of changes to come
Impersonal

Waves
A-wash
Upon hearts
Mortified –
O days;
Gone?
Or
To become?

જ&

Death of a Loser

So from my place
I get to say
So little here
I get by now
With so little
Hearing so few
Helping voices
From anywhere
I get to be
Now
On my own
I live
To die!
And, if I kill myself
Oh! Yes but you were
All so immaculate
In your dresses and all
While I just sat here
Immobilized
And getting nothing
I exist
To fail!
My failure
Is my Truth
That is within me
So, what you see
Is all a lie
Sweet imaginary
Friends
Out there
I write to you
All
In my own
Mind
I guess
You may have
Just existed
But it was
A little
Too late for me.

ॐ

Death of Inspration

Forgive them
Those who fall
Failing in their grasp
To touch beauty's breath

And so,
Tenderness suffers
From her abused brain
oxed so many times
By intending fists
Splintering without
Pause.

❧❦

Death Shall End Us All

Beauty says
You cry
Within yourself alone;
You stand
Near that mirror
And you still cannot know
What it is in you?

A smile painted
By an unknown artist, years ago
Explained your anguish
For all the unknown years that you have endured
And that
Years from now
You shall still endure

Tell, ye now, unto the Falling Ones;
The Innocent Dying Ones;
Tell the Sorrowful Ones
Ye Tormented Ones
Ye innocent Crucified Ones
Death Shall End In Us All
Death Shall End In Us All.

A silence booming
Heralding hope
A saviour between us
And coming beauties
Respecting serenities
Telling the colours
Of hatreds juxtaposed
And yet still meaningful –
Saviour and Protector
With your armies
Come and save us
For, Humanity, is wilting away
Beneath the mind crushing
Slices of our Sick Civilization

The cheerless violin of inexpressible yearnings begs me:
"Understand my tune!"
But how can I do this

When I am a mortal with indifferent
Passions?

Friend of mine, listen now, for what
Beauty says:
"The Weak of the Earth
"Cry in sadness
"And the Sad of the Earth
"Are around you
"And within you".

All of you humans
Are trying to speak lucid poetry
Poetry aghast at this life
"O! Where will we stand?"
I hear screams, shrieks and whispers all
Melting and repulsing each other
In confusing rackets and blares and stillness
"In years hence
"Where will we laugh?
"And where will we cease to be?"

Yes, you must desire those
Needs unfulfilled
Of yours
Must be nourished
In your bosoms

Between us all;
Hopeful Saviour, Protector does not abandon us!
I say to you:
May there be
Peace unto us all
And may there be stillness and closure
To our all sorrows.

ဆ

Decadence Preverse

Everyone talks
And experiences
And experiments
And gets confused
Depressed
And anxious

People fearful
With multiple sexual partners
While a baby is alone
Crying nowhere
As people smoke their drugs
And laugh
And they start to go
Nowhere
Some doing business
And living out empty lives

In a soulless planet
Christ!
I am really surprised by all of you people
Asking and questioning the same questions
Again and again and more
"Is there life out there?"
"Is there life in this universe?"
"Are we all alone?"
You keep on repeating your questions
And I ask you:
"Is there any life here on earth?"

I see a young girl suffering from torment
And hearing sorrow
Being riddled throughout her fragile mind
Is this, then, your civilization?
People!
You gamblers and prostitutes
Fraudsters and women beaters
Compulsive liars and addicts
Rich criminals, poor criminals
Slithering through your pointless slimy days
That we all know where it's all ending

Christ!
But one baby's life
Is never pointless!
I tell you so..

৪৩

Depression

A word, my friend, I heard
Where Angels of my Father's memories, spoke shockingly
Where Mother's weeping's sang dirges in my mind
I can never ignore these pages and essays that affect us brittle humans

And where upset throats hurt once more
The dryness wounds sincerely
How could a clown cry, I thought?
Here, and forever more, I thought - and for what meaningful end?

The Wilderness will forever be my life's highway!
Endless in repercussions and unsure threats vague
Where eyes conversed in sentences distracted and disconnected
Where body language denied the presence of all meanings or sense

I complained unto no one
For I did complain once unto a god I believed in once
A god I thought could change and alter physics and its grand laws
Yet dryness once more hurt my memory as I attempted
As I attempted and tried to recall what efforts I needed to do
Such as recalling images exact of my 'friends' that were meant to help me

I saw too many hollow, unoccupied, futile skies
'Neath which thorny verses of Sacred Scripture were passionately, lucidly preached
But I tried myself far removed and away
And turned aghast towards
Situations where lies convinced us of truths
Where lovers expressed intimacy within plasticity's contexts
Eventually, surrendering my sanity and soul
I myself simply stood and looked at snowy sands cold
That was all I existed for
To stand and watch you all live on.

ଚଚ

Destroyed Tombstone

Rain
Some weeping
Some obliterating
Storms
Angers of epochs 'cross centuries
Hollering hurt
Yet, unheeding you
Choose to live then

And when
Pressures are extreme
And
When Rocks cried
For you humans
That lie here
Scattered
You lie
With no epitaphs
Remaining
To dignify you
Perhaps you, the Living,
Watching these scenes here
Can think
From what those
The Dead
Chose to live out
Their lives?

Humans!
Yes, you!
Though beaten severely
Such a beating
Scattering your sinful blood
Fisting out
Your eyeballs
You humans!
Once alive with ardour!
Now departed
Way beyond what our
Remembrance can care for
And you, now
The Living
What thoughts may be composed

Within your breasts
As you think

An arc of Humanity
From Stonehenge to the Pyramids
To the Tower of London
Think, then;
Of those long, gone and Dead?
Feel the expanses of time
That therein exist

Humans scattered!
Butchered
Recall
Your loved ones
Once lurid, glitzy
And now, themselves
Also
Lie lifeless

And now behold
These Souls Scattered
With no tombstones
To recall
Their echoing lives;
So what now,
Ye Living Souls
Tell me, then
What whispers
You think of?

&

Destructive Confusion

People and a living life
Evaporates
Suddenly
You seek wise talk
Everything
Totality
Is spreading inwards
And confusion hates herself
Eating themselves up
Within this much
Factions hating factions
Within ourselves
Denying each other
These self hatreds continue
And continue
Fuelling their destructive worthlessness

We're eating up
Our fleshy knives
And we're just so slowly going
To our soggy graves
Here now

ॐ

Devil's Dream!

The Thousand Year Old Cathedral's sorrow
Whose eyes
Feel alone
Searching
For stillness
Amidst leaves
Scattering
Murmurs suggesting
That Death calls
You;
Your roads dance
Insane
Bewildering Nature
And her creatures
As Cruelty's hands
Speak inside
And for yourself
Expounding
Words' meaningless intents
Let sleep hover
Hover heavy now
'Neath winds undeciding
I scream!
Hope is nailed!
Love is finally nailed extinct!

ဒဝ

Die Within Your Life, and Therefrom Live

Goodnight
My watery Grave
That I
Breathe in

In my life
Is Nigh
This truth
That we live
To be
Endless drizzles
Spoken sentences
Of a lifeless truth
In beauty's hurt
Empty glamour
You all shall shrivel
Sweet life
The distances I see
Are fast approaching
My end
Pointlessly angering me
Children of the bleakest night
Fogs of indecency
Ugly eyes
Staring at your sensitivities
Scattering your smiles
Killing the unborn
Innocence's turning wild too soon

Laughs and cries
Tears and smiles
Uselessness is our essence
Read the epitaphs
That lie everywhere
So alive
Writing on their innermost truths
And an irrelevance we've all been
Didn't you know?
So finally die tonight
Within your own life
And therein you shall
Feel relief
From your expanding
Hurt.

ෝ

Discussin Your 'Self' With Your Self

1. *Faces can mix together*
    Sentences can become as one
    Though 'faces' you see seem to be different
    Are personalities all 'one'?
    Needing an essence we talk of endlessly
    Needing a purpose
    Purpose via a meaningful existence
    Meaningful existence via a sincere community
    That is profoundly sincere
    Wherein all creatures aspire hourly
    To be as humans
    For, listen, we are not born mentally human
    We must become that perfect human condition

2. *Yet, all too often conditions lash out at our fallible hopes*
    Strange shady situations murder our passionate needs
    Look around you
    Where meaningful speech is ridiculed
    Where 'friends' are usually no more than
    Convenient alliances
    Look around you
    The routinization of your existence
    Yes, one day you get a different job
    A different home
    A different city
    Yet, routinization is screaming working behind you
    Chasing you with much breath cursed to spare
    Look around you
    The lack of fulfilment inner
    The lack of nourishment
    The lack of genuine spirituality and innocent love
    That just does not exist within your life

3. *You hear of humans seeking their 'souls'*
    People seeking their 'selves'
    People listening to religions of the east
    Religions such as Buddhism
    And Zen
    People needing to be with their 'real selves'
    You do not hear the laughter, do you?
    You do not see the ridicule, do you?
    You are too immersed in your journey
    In your trek

But what is 'it' that you are looking for?
'My Self' you reply
Your search is in vain
A profound loss
It is your loss
Spent in tears that only you will experience and feel
For your 'self' is abstract
Your 'self' are memories indicting
Events
Sounds
Sceneries
Thoughts
Your 'self' is a random mixture that fluctuates
Your 'self' is a random changing mixture
Of sounds, sceneries, odours, events, memories, sounds
And nothingness's
Your 'self' is your present moment
Your 'self' is the particular and changing chemicals
In your brain

4. You seek your 'self'
While that 'self' is at your door
Your 'self' is an entity you actually know
There needs to be no 'search'
Your 'self' is within your mind now
This exact moment of now
Ask your 'self'
And your 'self' will reply
Your desires are all there
Ask about your hatreds
And your 'self'
Will tell you all about them

5. Yet, you fear your 'self', don't you
You fear the immediate knowledge that will be so available to you
Your meditations and your searching's and your years of efforts
And your years of anxieties and your years of terrible sorrows
And your years of not knowing is in truth
Delaying tactics by you because of the fear inhabiting you
For, your 'self' seeks a different self from what your real self is
Your searching
Is nothing but the attempt to recreate a different self
From what your real self is
And so you continue the lies
And your lack of fulfilment continues unabated

6. *Yourself is you this moment, I tell you!*
   Right now
   Your self are your potentialities now
   Your self are your capabilities now
   Right now, yourself knows exactly who you are
   Your self is you
   And your searching's and readings
   And meditations are externalizing your problems
   From your actual self
   Because you fear yourself, silly human
   Your fear what?
   You fear the unpleasant possibilities that lie within you
   'Unpleasant' possibilities
   Are your own judgements
   Remember
   My self-disconnected friendless friend

   ඥ

Distant Wisdom

1. For those who question
What words are meaningful to them
Those who need
Questions whose origins are practical to them
Yet, do not suffer sorrow, nor despair
Life's pauses, you must accept
For the vision in the distance remains
Awaiting thee
An oasis, real and final.

2. When some ask you of errors
Of indignities, of sadness
Do not turn inside
In search of answers
Answers of pain, answers of futility
Do not burn yourself
Your one heart beating
Stillness defined much wisdom
Stillness, the twin sister of Patience was wisdom's bride
Yes, many suffer
Many grieve
Of itching and flagrant wounds
Of obscene and frightful deformities
Of faces you no longer recognize
Yes, many are chained
Their limits are defined
Bear the hatreds within your chest
Restrain the deeds for the proper hour
Otherwise, spent you shall be
Spent, as the lost leaf falling
Guided by the whims of an uncaring wind
Think, then, of where you shall fall
Think, then, of how hard you would fall.

3. The shambles of History
The follies of conversations
The dullness of so many minds
Breathe this air you breathe
Contemplate the thousands of those before you
For, you are not alone
What you undergo has been repeated
Repeated in the self-same shambles of History
History!

History is the history of Man
The history of You
From dictators and their pawns
To yawning democracies
Whose subjects are equally dead
How then, do people ignore it?
When a soldier suffered of thirst choking in some century
And another soldier suffered the same in another century
Where does the difference lie?

4.   In your life, you recognize repetitiveness
Recognize, then, history's repetitiveness
Understand therefrom
And what do you say to the one who cares not for hope?
For those forced on the streets of wilderness and decay
What do you say to those whose culture is vice?
Distant as you are
Or, close as you are to them
Or one them you may be
What words do you say?
The spark must arrive
The spark for organized movement
One that involves them
That is for their guidance
Therefore, unto the streets you too must journey
Unto the streets of decay and into their hearts
Say a world of vast superiority can exist
A different world
A world of harmony can be
That is all
To feel that thought is the key
For, few believe it
Few care
Soul's forgotten
Themselves, they forgot!
Themselves, they killed!
In life's myriads
In life's experiences
And varied and incomprehensible emotions
In life's sudden dullness
The shocks
Take heed
Understand the oceanic ignorance that exists
Understand your enemies
Understand the existence of fools and idiots

The existence of human insects
Understand the existence of torturers who smile genuinely
Of poets, who understand little
Understand the existence of the varieties of human beings
Then, you shall never allow your heart
To hear the words and feelings of surprise
Understand the depths of those who stand before you yesterday, today and tomorrow.
Understand their cravings
Understand their real intentions, motivations and desires
These are the humans
Of which, you may be one
For every human seeks your Anguish

5. Sigh carefully, then
Sigh understandingly, what battalions you face
Understand the nature of the hidden gunfire aimed at you
Understand the decoys aplenty
Within that context, exist to expand justice and permanent equality
Exist, to help the lonely
Exist, to help the pained one
The crying one
The sufferers; the chained; the blinded
The deafened; the mutilated; the abused;
The raped; the beaten; the ignored one
Souls forgotten
Soldiers unknown
What path did they take?
What passions did they have?
What thoughts crossed their minds?
Souls forgotten
Throughout this world
Suffering in silence
Suffering in loneliness
Who will touch them?
Who will shelter them?
Where are you all tonight?
Ye ghosts from the deeds of idiotic, uncaring humans
Who decided on your fatal fates?
When?
And for whom did you once cheer
When your existence was being decided upon?

6. Souls forgotten!
I tell you, you are no different than forgotten soldiers
All have been trampled upon

All have been abused
Daily and hourly
And in their remembrance,
And in your to-be remembrance
You shall all be forgotten!
As the unknown martyred soldiers have been forgotten
Forgotten by the dust of their remains
By skulls deliberately fractured
By the scattered limbs
Truths do exist
Yet, truth's greatest enemy
Is Ignorance.

৪৫

Do Not Despair

Speaking eyeless child
Your heat is hearing
Of Murmurs
Saddened
By Refusals categorical
And why
Beautiful death
Do you exorcise
Yourself within my faint Life?
In times forsaken
Christ's have turned Mad
I discovered
Our lyrics were hallowed and bitter
Unto you I spoke
Here
Baby aghast
So soon?
Unto whom did you understand then?
Forget grammar and forget politesse
We are here in our world
In our testing and trying times
Speak to us then
Beauty deformed
Utters mismanaged feelings
Mismanaged hope being bought
Deformed flowers being raised
Again by entities labelled by names futile and irrelevant
Irrelevance we all are
Existing in dust
Harmonies within themselves splashing contradictions
Women of openness speaking trash
Trash of innocence
The trash of the Foolish
Fools who happen
To Rule our Daily Lives
And the Fools in love
I hate them all, I confess
Hatred in mine eyes
Competing wildernesses
Telling me beauty can never be defined
And are you listening, you insecure ones?
Are you scared?

Wearied by your smiles
Tell the ruling rapist
To die sincerely
Killers schizophrenic and aloof
Exterminate them greedily
Mother!
Look at me hurting grievously before you
Do not weep, I tell you
Tell your children sorrowful
Not to despair
Life offers more!
Yet, in us
With us
Within you
Speak not hollow feelings
And never be
Unpoetical in the midst of
Your sorrow.

ᎧᏧ

Do You Or Do You Not Understand?

How many tears does it take to spell my 'hurt'
For You?
Will it ever be that my painted and written words,
Express unto your heart
A sincerity of whatever value of some decent Worth?

I am fragmented
That is true
I write my truths that may not be altogether
Coherently viable
Sweet child, but
I do not lie
I write my truths

I write just for you, the One
Do you not perceive?
Tell me if it is beyond your comprehension
So then, I shall cease my seemingly vain efforts
Of talking and loving and expressing my ardent
Longing
For you
To be with me
Will you?
Or no?

∾

Don't Deny Me

Sweet
Baby boy
What beauty
Can be
In you
I see
Innocence
Screaming his
Needs
I see
I see
Laughter from the shyness
In you
Come, then, to me
I'm your protector
Forever to be
Don't you then
Deny me
As I unfold here
And shrivel
In my final years

৪৩

Don't Worry If You Should See Me

And if normality were to come back to me
So suddenly
A beauty to be
In my real life
To help me
Can that really be?
Because
I have become rather
Brittle
Didn't you know?
Now you ought to know
Friends of mine
That I no longer really know
Any of you;
The sadness
In my years
And in the sick oceans of my life
Have been
Far too exhausting
So, don't you worry too much
If you should see me
It may all come back to me
After all, I've lost it all through my own
Mismanagement
No?

ॐ

Dysfunctional Mind

Your eyes I don't wish to see
An eye-ball evaluates me
No Body knows me
The sceneries change too fast
Unknowing to people
The streets are moving ahead
Winding in and in
Unexpectedly
I'm trying to be
But what's to 'be'?
Where is it to 'be'?
Who's compassion?
Searching in Art
Searching Humanity
Searching somewhere
And getting
Awfully Polite
Rejections

ভেভ

Dysfunctioning Life

Passing by groaning graves
Stillness hushes now!
What once was Furious party
Lives of splendour and decadence
Now lie solemnly dead
Think, of your minds, I feel
Think, of your emotions, I feel
Where they been?
And so, think now, of where they now stand?

The severely sad
Are struggling now to cope
Fearing suicide
And yet,
Fearing life itself more

What a planet!
What a world!
Beauties of models, clubs, yachts, parties, mansions
Cripples of despised ones, hated ones, dry ones
Listening to me;
Where is all going, where is all being?
Where is it all, your civilization and Humanity?
I wonder?

When we listen
To nothing
And no one
Educates us of the worthlessness
Of what we're indulging in
Do you know the Price you will surely pay?

What then are the 'rules' for your life?
What are the 'guidelines' for your principles?
Is anyone there to tell me?
Or are we born naked here
To live without reason?
Where are the Blessed ones?
Where are the just, Loving ones?
Where are the faithful, Compassionate ones?
Where are the dedicated, Faithful ones?

I'm still searching for you
Trustworthy ones
But from the rest of you all
I'm going to do one thing;
I am
Seeking to disentangle myself from you
From this filth
From myself
From my dysfunctional existences.

છ

Emergency Case

Face turns down
An eye sees
Suddenly it feels
A revelation unto itself
And the decay is outside
And the danger is outside
The intents I'm seeking
The intents I'm looking at
All of you
You there
You're talking
You're loving
Why?
Ask yourselves now
In this lonely quiet hour
Ask your selves
A human
Becomes a pop-Lichtenstein painting
A human becomes a comic book
A human becomes a drowning stink
A human becomes bubble gum pop-manufactured idiot
A human acts a role
Believes in the 'role'
Clown criminal role
Can you like that human?
An emergency case dies
No food
No money
Was discarded
Buried somewhere
I'm here
You're there
There's the equation
I'm my experiences
You're, your experiences
Let's communicate here, now.

ෆෂ

Emotions of a Burdened Woman

If I feel
My tears
Rupturing

And if I feel
My fractured language
To be hollow

I am
Seeming to be seen
By you
But in reality
I know
That I am really
Nowhere

I am
An
Inert being
That has no gravity

You did punish me
Your people
Did beat me
Enough
Don't you think?
I have had enough
Or should I have more

Of your stinging rage
Against me
But you never understand
Or understood
That I did nothing
And that I am innocent

These are my words
Written for my Babies
And to you
Anyone out
There
Who may read my
Words
These words
Express feelings
And feelings
Express pain
That really burns.

❧

Empty Human

I was never too sure
If I was right
Or wrong
These were just abstractions to me
My mind of Nothingnesses
I loved this one
Or that one
What did I know?
About all of them
I knew nothing
That was *my* truth
But I didn't know
My own truths
You see

I lived
I breathed
I continued to produce
Manufactured thoughts
Manufactured opinions
That I then
Believed were to
Be truths
And then guess what
I defended these manufactured stones
And I became passionate
For them
Idiot man Ayad
How can stones
Ever be passionate?

I dressed this way and more
And did talk in this style
But what was it all to mean
I thought
It meant so much
But it meant
Simply nothing
I was a nothingness
Living in a world of
Abstractions
Where in the end
Emptiness was

The grand net result
Created between us all

I went to university
And I learned the
Philosophies of stupidities
Yes, my God
How I never even managed to learn
These philosophies
Of Nothingnesses.

ॐ

End of Another Pointless Night

12.07AM
Try to feel
Try to believe
In our world
Where we are nothing at all
Kill the bird
Out of anger
Your muddled burden
We can all see
Don't lie to yourself

It is now officially April 11th, Thursday, 1991...

Where's Cho?
Lonely
And dead
Be tired
Weary eyes
Dead already?

You fool
You're condemned
In yourself
In us
In whoever

ɕɞ

Enough, Please.

Please help me
Whoever you all may be
Yes, if you need me to,
I can give
My heart
That lies exhausted
Burning out
It's all an ending
For myself
Yes
I'm losing
My 'life'
That I never experienced
My slaughtered soul
Who has decided to die
Sir, Ma'am
I'm going out
Now
You've seen
My pathetic pages
That have been rightly read
By no one
Well, what does it matter now?
Christ?
Are you there?
Your pouring blood
Satisfied no one
Everywhere and no one
While, I breathe still
While I am
Being hounded by abnormal fears
That threatens me,
Sir, God
That threatens my entire Existence
Please now
Please, either decide to
Forgive me
Or tell me to end my sickening life
I think
Sir
I've been hurt
Quite enough

I think I've been
Destroyed
Enough
Beyond belief
I think I've just had enough
Of all of this
'Life' of Perpetual Panic
Here
And now
I plead unto you:
What more do you
Want from me?

જાજ

Essences I Feel

Hearing
Smiles lasting
Times twisting
In aches
Painful
Turning mindless
Away, you're away
Travels involuntary
To where?
To where?
A scream I've felt
Scream that frightened me
Widespread panic
Humanity hurting
Poverty unjust
What are you hearing?
In us
A community
Community of ethics
We're flying
Far, far away
You're all far, far away
Help me
Gather closer
Where I can feel
Where I can touch
Turn these screams melodious
In moments euphoric
I see horizons of serious and joyous Art
Where I see passions turned eternal true
Turn a hand to me
The essences I feel
I swear this life
Can be so much more
This life can be so much more.

৩৫

Evening's Fragrance

A child weeps
Her harmonies I paint
Her eyes
Their pain twisting
I write
As her mind crumpled
In despair
I speak of
Childless soul!
Your rain
You weep
Dew in your essence
I feel depths here
As you suffer
My eternal image
You are,
Flame of my heat
Truth of my sadness.
Reveal to me, then
Your final tears,
Drain me
As I watch you
Evaporate gently
Loneliest child
That I ever did see.

෨෬

Falling Into My Death

Tell me, in your eye
My own letters
That, yes
Are so wrong;
I know.

For, they were
Written only when I was
So inflated
By my manic intoxicated mind.

I tell you
This is:
My being!
The same Being that has
So gone astray;
Flying apart from
My unknowing Self

And I go on
Falling
Frighteningly so
For remember
Just how much
I fear heights
As I continue
Plunging
Into an unknown
That I far prefer
To end my life
Than to ever see through its end

For, you must understand
That I much need to experience
The Quicker End
I called
Suicide
Rather than go through
The Long End
I called
My Life

ဆ

Fatal Flaws

People that are forced to be sarcastic
At their pointlessly bloody and empty lives
Suffer from low pay
And seriously heavy stress
Smoking frantically endlessly
Women are being raped
Life is fraught with
Lies and insecurities
Overcrowded jobs
That can be taken from you tonight
Just while you peacefully sleep

Pollution and incest
I tell you the truths are being
Murdered by the atheist priests
That are preaching
Endless sermons
To empty rooms

The people
Of this
Rich land
England
Are hurting
Suffering from exasperating loneliness
While we laugh drunkenly

Listen to the pontificating liar
He is telling us how to live
And the millions
Are listening

While the failures
Like my self
Have no more
Evocative words
To rouse
Anyone

After all
Isn't Failure a fatal
Medicine?

ॐ

Fatal Mistake

Forgiveness
A heart speaks of the mistake
Of her Passion
Accursed mistake!

Who can ever help now?
For life's evening subsides
Gently, leaving

Forgiveness!
Why do you stand there
Like a statue
While you weep
For others, unknown to you?

I tell you this
Still
Her Beauty was Unmatched
I say this forever
Her Beauty
Was unmatched forever.

&

Feelings Of A Happy Woman

I was never too sure
If I was right
Or wrong
These were just abstractions to me
My mind of Nothingnesses

I loved this one
Or that one
And what did I know
About all of them?

I knew nothing
That was my truth
But I didn't know
My own truths
You see
I lived
I breathed
I continued to produce
Manufactured thoughts
Manufactured opinions
That I then
Believed were to
Be truths
And then guess what?

I defended these manufactured stones
And I became passionate
For them
Idiot man
How can stones
Ever be passionate?

I dressed this way and more
And I did talk in this style
But what was it all to mean
I thought
It meant so much
But it meant
Simply nothing
I was nothingness
Living in a world of
Abstractions

Where in the end
Emptiness was
The grand net result
Created between us all

I went to university
And I learned the
Philosophies of Stupidities
Yes, my God
How I never even managed to learn
These philosophies
Of Banality.

ↁↁ

Feelings On Our Mortality

How brittle
Is life
A quivering dependence
On fragilities
And never on God
Where did our soulful appeals
To Him all end up and go?
Do you think God will
Allow us to
Proceed
Or not
That's the answer
To our perpetual woes
This day
Our grief is washed
While tomorrow
It shall turn to
Brief joy
And joy
Then returns
To its abode
Of everlasting sorrow
And that is the guideline
Of the path
The God that we know nothing of
Has chosen to
Build for us
Wether
We wished it or not
Deepest suffering
Is our
Burden and that
Is a life
He
Has painted for us
A film, yes
A brief film indeed.

కుం

First World Lady Versus Third World Human

1. *And if a truth were to be alive*
For 'you';
Would you 'believe' it?
And if you did believe it,
Then would not you exist thereby too?
Since truth is by your definition
'Existence' –
Then whatever you may believe in
Will make you too to be 'real', no?

2. *You are Who'?*
You are an entity with a collection
Of contrasting and emerging
And convoluted and contradictory
And mutually attracting
Traits and characteristics
You call 'emotions'
Can you actually ever
Tie them up
Into some form of unified mental situation
Or is it impossible?

3. *And there we have 'you'*
'You' are a packaged entity
Varying and changing too
Indefinable and ultimately meaningless
In their essential constituents
So, then, from a mass of nothingness's
Evolves a form that is recognizable
That we humans recognize as being 'you'

4. *You love*
This person
But I inform you that you're intoxicated
With this other 'human'
Love is the mental situation
Of being drunk with passion
For any other moron
And that is why marriage and relationships hurt so much
It is because, soon
Your intoxication will inevitably wear off
And you will be left with the horror
Of being with a gigantic insect

That makes you feel sick
And yet
Since you declared to the wide world how much you love him
You are now – just for now – stuck
With this deformed, hairy cockroach
You feel desperation as you feel

5. There's too much turbulence in your imagined relationship
Fine
And then what?
What are you going to do with this blob of
Sickening flesh?
You break up
And you cry pain
Then
You seek a job
Did you study?
Did you qualify for anything?
Yes or no?

6. For those who answer 'Yes'
You go this way
And for those of you
Who answered 'no' you go the wrong way

7. You get a job
Great
But your job doesn't quite get to pay your
Rent and your electricity bills
And your gas bills
And your tax bills
And your telephone bills
And your food bills
Are unanswered
So now what?
You are angry
You live in a democracy
But you are voiceless
That's the greatest trick democracies
Play on you naive creatures
You are non-entities
You, the sad of the earth
You think your votes count
For something

But I tell you your votes and your voices
And your protests count for null and naught and void

8. *You look at third world countries*
And you think those dogs live in medieval times
Really?
But how about you?
What power do you have?
What influence do you have?
Who controls your lives?
Do you know?
Or do you think you are
I-N-D-E-P-E-N-D-E-N-T?
You are not
You are nothing but miscarried, dwarfs
You are puppets, my friendless friends
But you do not think so
You think you are 'free' individuals
In your first world lives

9. *You think if you speak words against your leaders*
That means, you are free
You think if you protest and scream
That means you are free
That proves to you
That you live in
A free society
You do not live under a dictatorship
No, only third world countries
Are dictatorships
You live in a dictatorship without
Dictators
In your First World Western world

10. *God bless you!*
I just wish I could be living like you!
But I need to talk to you
If you want to listen, that is
You, in the great civilised First World countries
Like the US, Canada, Europe, Australia
Live under dictatorships
What is the difference then
Between the dictatorships of the First World and the Third World?
Here it is:
In the Third World, the Dictatorship is obvious

It stands in front of you
If you do not obey, you're done with
While in your happy First World
You can do as you please
But as long as you never, ever
Dare to touch the frontiers of the powers that control
Your nations

11. Your minds are castrated
By the retarded mass media
By your movies
Your television
Your education
By your socialising with your empty-headed 'friends'
Who will gladly trample on you
Whenever they feel there's a need for them to do so

∞

Sons of Adam

When I am
In this hour that stares at me
And whenever I speak
I turn and pluck out my brain
Into shrivelled fragments of frightened pain
This end
Is my beginning
From this dim, icy room
I eat my life
Within and throughout
I just invite you all
But I'm getting nowhere
In my own attempts
To live with you all
Sons of Adam

ೞ

Baby Izzet

Sweet son
Listen then to my
Dreams
That have been
So far and away
In lands of awful yonder
And more
Trust my heart
Young one
Trust my only heart
That flaps
For one day
You, too, shall see
These hellish truths that I have been
Through
My young boy
I tell you, Son
The shocked winds will speak of frenzied twists
Within history's painful passions
Brought on
By none else
Except us mortals here
On this sorry land
Of ours
Young boy;
My eternal love
Listen, then, if you can
Listen to my soul's breathing
Palpitating
Izzet
No one else shall care
For you
So much
As I did
Izzet
No one
Can care for
You
As much
As I did.

☙❧

Cold Cave

A guitar lonely strummed
Itself
Awakened its feelings
Its feelings varied and the obscure
Its feelings rebellious
Its feelings hungry
Alone, it heard a voice
A voice preaching to her self
The situation meant something
Absolutely something, I think
And laughter was heard
When a monk declared himself the latest messiah
The god we've all not been waiting for
Yet, listening to the non-entities
Their charmless weight
Weighing heavily on me
Obscuring me
Delaying me
Depriving me
Who is society?
Who are the atoms
Who are opinionated?
Who sincerely believed
They understood
Anything?

A blind woman drew me to a soft cave
A cave hidden
Hidden from humans
In kit were rough inscriptions ancient and unknown
I saw them
"Read them to me, you fool!" asked the lady
I never realized her darkness till then
I read the inscriptions ancient
"Turn alone"
"Turn wilderness profound into yourself"
"Alight hands; only hands that are giving"
"Understand the blindness of Man"
"Understand Man's worthlessness"
"Realize Man's deeds"
"So preach to those whom you understand."
"Understand Man's lyrics"
I cried!
'This was written when?'
The blind woman replied:
'Sixteen thousand years ago!'
The forests were coldened
The rains stormed on us
Where we were hidden in our ancient cave
The storm whistled its destructive desires at that particular moment
And alone we were
Myself and the blind woman
There we understood nothing
Nothing existed between us
Nothing at all.

&c.

For What It May Mean, May Not Be Clear To You

Don't listen to the sounds of truth
Where vagabonds spelled their needs
In words inscribed by fingers of shame
You may well be too hurt by it all!
Come here, my old ones
Friends and Death!
So do you seem forever apart
For the final wink has just arrived
I think so
And what it may mean, may not be clear to you
The trial of your sickness has begun
Justice is coming to you
While your jury you have murdered
For then, who shall pronounce judgements and verdicts
Or so you may really think

ဆဒ

Forget Humanity

In towns, appearances vague
The walker smiled smiles futile
Only he could describe unto himself
A waste was deserted into plights of wilderness common
And the poverty-stricken wept laughter at themselves, you could not hear
As the sighs weep in the tales heroic to me
For me
Loneliness private I describe
In nights starless hiding in their memories' luggage
Where else can existence become, I asked you all
The retarded dancers frightened the innocent ones, full of blame
The horrors attached themselves to scathing instances
While profound thinking beauties sorrowed and despaired
I ask questions blue and tangled
Where did melancholy originate?
The wise soul, student of Humanity, inquired
In hours of haste and insecurity, that we call existence
O but didn't you hear
That love and warmth and touch did die earlier this evening
Your letters of passionate reasoning never did reach anyone
In your scattered voice I only heard you once in front of me
No, you never did you really write back to anyone
So why blame me
My wild attempts at success were wild failures
Don't scream at my screaming heart
Where murderous nails promoted the unbeatable
Hardness and insatiable Cruelty of Man
Man of the greasiest hatreds
What did you ever appreciate in me
In my twists, yes I did love the some
In their hallowed and angelic
They composed
Scriptures of Being
Symphonies of the sublime, joy and awe to God
But, far too often
Far too often for my fluctuating brain
I saw and experienced little more
Desolations disquieting me
Yes, I sensed some distant truths and meanings
But what use did I gather therefrom?
In my existence
Yes, I did see, again and again

The burdened hopeless weeping the blackest tears
For the Ancient and Modern History
Of Man, the peaceful, the compassionate – the sickest bastard of them all!
Now, I say to you all, farewell, goodnight
Unto God, may we meet
In peace and in serenity pure
So will all the dreamers
In overcrowded prisons of your unquiet minds
Where all you feel and smell are hatreds despairing
No one ever understood us
And so, we shall leave them behind us
Farewell humans of mass murder, endless deceits and easy betrayals
Humans of sweatiest, filthiest lust against the innocent ones
Humans of persistent lies, obsessive back stabbing, fanatical thievery
And abuse and exploitation of Satanic proportions
You gave us nothing
But mass extinctions and brutal force
Never once did we see justice and fairness!
May God have mercy on you all
Though, I doubt it.

இஇ

Frustrations

What did they tell me
Their eyes that explained nothing
Your empty cries of 'Liberation' that were heard around
In the gatherings of orphans who pleaded to be your twins
And what did they tell me
As I grew up
In your world
In years early and damp
Unstructured brains that were daily washed
By the Hands of Sin
You people are becoming abstract
Masses and faces
Yet all needing
Needing and belonging
To the faces and masses
Whilst everyone
Ignores each other.

వావ

Fugitive From Injustice

Welcome me into your Life!
Welcome me into your Mind
The one
That rejected my angry Life
And her repressed Soul;
Will you welcome me then
Today?
Because –
Because it is so cold
This strange dawn of yours,
It burns with a freezing
Hatred
Lashing out at my terrified smile
That will try
And try still
To exist
In this bewildering World
Of yours.
Welcome me, then, please
In this arctic climate of yours
Where polite protocol
Means more than poverty's needs
Where irrelevant conversations
Mean more than starving anxieties
Please!
Welcome me
Somewhere
Because you see
In truth, I can no longer
Run from you;
By now I am trying to run
From my own breaking Self
That, yes, has so much
Failed me
In this your
Planet of Freezing Lives.

ॐ

Gala Awards for Pedophiles

And many times
I did, hope
Many times, I've meant to speak
But where exactly is the use of it all?
For 'use' was far – too far away
While uselessness killed me here
I tried to expand my mind
To meet the beginnings of love
But how useless
I screamed
Everyone's a criminal in his
And her
Own way
And you know that yourself
This, then, is the existence of the meandering river
Somehow we find ourselves
Within it all
Within the parties and conferences and meetings
Of social criminals
And gatherings of women beaters
And charities for child abusers
We've got to smile
Shake hands and act sincere!

ೞ

Give Up Giving

Come to give
And you'll live
This life
From an
Uncertain trial
Of sarcastic jurors
Whose only concern
Are painful recollections
Scattered by
Hungry, vengeful
Lovers
So, give up giving
My soul
And live life
Therefrom.

God – Please Give Me Peace?

1. I am deaf as a door knob
Blind as darkness
And mute as a pebble
I am disabled by persecuted luck
Wherever I go
And whatever I try to do
I break down

2. I know really well
What constitutes myself
Are fragmentary entities
Hating each other
And that makes me
Crippled in my mind
And in my behaviour
I hope you are understanding
My words and their heat?

3. I wake each morning feeling happy
And then
That first flicker of madness
Really hits me
Telling me
This new day
Will be like
All your yesterdays
And then, I ask myself
'What am I to do with my life?'

4. I have two choices
Either to go and suffer your torture
Or I end my sickening life
And I see myself continuing
In this 'Life' that is Hell for me
I do not need people
I do not need friends
I do not need family
For, you see, I have none
I never did have any
And before you feel 'pity' for me
Let me tell you quickly
I have no 'need' for family
Friends, lovers or any humans

5.   I cannot go outside my house
The house I do not even own by the way
Anyway, I cannot go outside
Why?
Because I have yet another disease
Fear of the vast expanses of space
How idiotic it sounds to you, I do know
But there you go, I've got that damned disease
As well
And so I must remain at my home, inside

6.   Because
We are the *Sick*
That is what God has wished for us
We are isolated
Because we embarrass you
And I am embarrassed to be with you
Normal souls
That is why we have to be isolated
There's Logic even in Madness!

7.   'Who' can help me?
No one
Is there any medications for my brain?
No there are no medications for my brain.
Why is that no one helps me?
Because no one can help me
So I am alone to face the Panic
On my own

8.   What is this 'fear' I keep talking about?
I don't want to talk about it
Actually it is because I cannot talk about it
Because
Whenever I talk about it
I feel the Panic will return against my mind

9.   How can I communicate with you?
We are so far apart
And, to be truthful
You are so lucky not to understand or feel
What I have to go through ever day in
My sick life
Christ, I wish I could live your life!

10. When I am in my car

And we are driving towards the highway
This fear is beyond words
I need, I feel, I have to smash my forehead
Against the window door
To create severe blood
In order to 'stop' the
Threat of Panic from bubbling
Into a Reality

11. When I was in a train, once
The Threat of Panic bubbled in myself
I felt the only way to
Extinguish that F.E.A.R. was to
Open the door of the running train
And for me to throw myself out
From my seat and onto
The moving rail tracks
And thereby my Death
Would end the agonising Torture
The emanates from
The 'mere' Threat of Panic
Through my Death

12. I am talking of the mere
'Threat of Panic'
Imagine how frightening that is
And imagine what a real, full blown Panic
Attack would do to me?
Christ, how am I to function in this life
That you, my Lord, gave me?
Or, perhaps, you are insinuating that
I should sever the arteries of my Life?

13. These are my serrated words
These are my jagged words
What do I mean by 'Ravaged Words'?
I mean I have been shredded through
Splintered, battered by my own
Uneasy, sick brain
That is fanatically determined to
Nail me at every second that I dare to
Breathe
Why?
Why, my God?
You chose that I have to be
Slaughtered and bruised
Way beyond belief
Or, way beyond human belief
Can comprehend

ᘒᘔ

Hallowed Night

Live now
As you try
From your only wisdom
That tries
So to gather her
Fruits
That once stood
So rejected
Tonight
Blue night
Shall explain her miseries to you
And in a strange twist
Lovers may yet
Agree
In their lies
And we may all be soothed
In our endless attempts
Of inner self-deceptions.
Sweet beginners!
Come to lie here
In between the truths
And her shades
This moment
May be fake
I guess

As I bleed here
In my echoes
I may bleed
My son!
That I need
Don't betray me
Now
My daughters!
Don't abandon me
As I write
My words
Human passions
Wherein we may
All
Live
And be;
Wherein
We may all
Be
And
Feel
Free.

Handwritten Words of a Misguided Woman

A silence dictates
Its hopes essential
That thirst in their intertwined
Hatreds for the
Struggle to breathe
The crowds staggered in their plodding
The howls turned nowhere
Even though they themselves
Really felt that their words
Had so many depths
But at least some flocks did hear these sounds
There was some heat generated
I say I heard roses
Crying gases inert
Their real feelings were soon discoloured
Did you ever understand
The ways and means
Of people?

I heard of clowns dying by suffocating themselves
Quietly
Didn't they at least
Entertain themselves?
I saw humbled and determined gatherings
Of angry frustrated citizens
But they soon were to hear
The words
Of misunderstood monks
Who finally produced a smile
But their words
Did ramble on and endlessly on
And the winds of their spirits
Were far too directionless
To be of any meaning

Then I saw Hurt
I saw engines crying
They spoke meaningless melodies to me
And I did try to guess
But I screamed
"You engines!" I screamed
"You can never sing, you maniacs!"
My brain

I felt was losing
Its functions
I wasn't too sure of what functions they were supposed
To do actually
Did you know what those functions
Were supposed to do?
I was not walking straight
And I knew it

Tell me of your cooking
I've been hungry for too long
You see
Or, you may see
It's been too long
And your language destroyed me here
My appetite was killed as well

And your subtle hatreds
Yes, I remembered them all
And I will repay you real for real
What you gave me
I shall give back to you

While a hopeful clown
He
And she
Entertained and spoke in dialects misunderstood
I swear peacefully
I even saw smoke pretending to be wisdom
Emanating from your breaths
That gunned me down
Down to my protecting ribs
I never have ever
Seen hatreds like these
I confess to you
The units of my poetry have gone mad
And my sense of geometry
Have turned ridiculous
As I lost my paths in my life
No, I agree
I never hated as much as you did
But I am catching up fast with you all
I never guessed
What predicaments Man can debase himself into
And then again

I never realized
What a lowly depth, I too could be forced into
I was stunned
I cried
My name is 'Ayad'
I thought that was enough
To convince criminals of my innocence

I was not misunderstood
That was incorrect
I was actually understood, quite well
Truth was
Nobody wanted to feel my truth
The speed of life
And human interactions and conversations
Easily bewildered me
And misguided me
I was tempted by the flowers of literature
I was tempted
When I saw independent women
Laughing joyously
I believed
There can exist a time
When loving can exist
In its sheltered solitude
Wherein there exists no indignities
Imagine
That your father
Is never berated
Imagine your mother
Is never to be shouted at
Rational fantasies or stupidities?

But then
The skies did change their colours
And meanings changed
And with the change of meanings
Intentions did change
Unto whom did the skies turn to?
And where did all the meanings of
Of every philosophy become?
Unto whom did they turn to?

෨෬

Harvard Sqaure Days

June 21, 1993 – London

You run from this house
Where we all belonged
In that instance
Where you used to be
So real
Old child
Singing so Still and Stiff
Maturing far, far too fast
Trying to catch the prosperous, joyful breeze
Of a fragrant revolutionary mind
Yes, though it was
Out there, in the desolations of No-Man's-Land
Wherein we all wore our glamorous uniforms
In their various serious disguises
Preaching holiness when, in truth
We ourselves were laden with Stones
And while fanatically pontificating
We were, in ourselves, desperately
Bitter from the worms of our own Insecurities
Screaming and seriously pleading
For a universal equality and a bearded youth
Long haired and anti- money
Anti the professors
Anti culture
Anti society
Anti values
Anti morality
Anti power
Anti the planet itself
And all you women
We told you about 'Womanhood'
And all those 'Curiosities' we tried to define
In between these oppressive contexts
Of our boring texts
We were ultimately and so sadly forced to live within
Our emerging pathos
Trying to breathe
In between the drunken supposed art scenes
And loose bowel arguments
Based on the last chemicals and random emotions

Lurching in your vague brains
"Let's all live communally again!"
"No more poor and rich"
We're all Equal"
"In serious togetherness"
And so our chants trudged on and on
Creating Cosy feelings about our Smug Selves
And the van Goghian 'Art Community Concept'
So what happened out there?
In romantic Harvard Square as we hung out
Not a care in this world
Except the starving billions
And how we hated while we loved
And through love sought the long distance overthrowing
Of every power that was
But in truth we threw over nothing more than
Our self-frying brains from reality
But then the bills were coming in too quick
And others had real airplanes to catch back home to their palaces
And we were soon all
Nowhere
To be found
Anymore

&

Hatred

From my own
Crusted eyes
They that
Blind
Themselves
In an endless
Hatred
I can only
Begin
To believe
In myself
Just
As I
Die.

&

Hermit's Words

I give
To forget
From my life
Of a forgotten
Denial

Can you now
Be in this heart
That soon
Shall cease
Her clapping?

৪৫

Hope

The beginning of
A smile
Is Hope

☙

Hopeful Soul

Come to speak, then to me
If you may
Children are being so hurt
Living in rotten, invisible areas
So near to you
And crying in their lonely sleep
Come to me
Children
And tell me, then, of your chilly ills
Maybe, just maybe
This darkened, hardened night
Can save you
The fading ones
You are somehow trying to reach me
And I to you
Come now
My beauties
I tell you
The sinners are your carers
And though you may still not
Understand much
You must react to my feelings for you.

❧

Hopeless Life

Believing in an age fading out beyond
See the pointless papers
Wisdom's broken literature;
Where governing insanity
Knocks unannounced at your lives;
Where figures of fighting birds
Escape for skies wherein there is greater freedom –
Understand the hungry one
And her smiles
Therein lies breathing wisdom I tell you!
Seeing the midst of a changing twilight
Can you ever imagine
In all the dry scenes, bitter experiences
You once imagined and felt
Can turn to voluptuous roses?
Crucified lover!
Upon your eyes blackened dreadfully so,
Do you wish to see anymore?
I plead for you to respond to my insecure soul!
Depraved dull routines
You live within
Irrelevance of language and expressions
Unfortunately
These are the words
That are being written
For no one
Though truly we live them!

෧෬

How Can I Understand That Which Is Undefined

Girl is lost again and is that a crime?
But for you, it is a 'crime'
And so you scream at her abuse and verbal excrement

Colours of emotions are confusing
Which one is which
Which is sincere and which is not
Touches deep
In sensitivities
While others equally
Hurt, debasing you

Where are you going?
What to where?
Who's to where?
And the same old random romances repeat themselves
Ad infinitum
As jolly drinks become dry
And initial sparkles cease to be anymore

Lost girl
Seeking silky winds
And friendly eyes
And profound hope
Distant
That is what I see
Distances far too expansive
Far beyond your reach

Hunger
Shining fists
Glowing against you
What can you believe in
When will sorrows cease
When will daybreaks proclaim
Serenity and peace and defiance eternal

You'll understand
What we feel
Elevated and serene
Dreaming passionately
Harmonies can be
Love can be
For the evolving girl-child
Begging through her smashed tears
To the innocent imprisoned ones
Asking for an answer
Within us all can be
Within us all can be

৩৫

Man Does Not Live by Bread Alone

I live
From what
Jesus told me
It's what spoke, Sire;

"Man does not live by bread alone!"
Fine, words you speak
But Sire; for I do not even have
'Bread' that you speak of

Sire, if you may, listen to my
Temperature
I possess
No money, home nor friends

Jesus My Beloved Sire
I lost my children
I live in a fanatical Panic,
That Obsessively
Is determined
To rip out and slice off my
Remaining mind, flesh and nerves

For it is not only I that speaks to You
Sire,
Look at us here, below your glistening, nailed Body
We, who choose to gaze at Your tortured mind
We, that some called 'Humanity'
We have nothing here within our depressed lives
Nothing

It is not only bread or food, if that is what you mean
That, yes, we do 'need' to live;
We have no security, no protection
No laws to protect us from prisons
Beatings, torture
No one to protect us Sire
From abject poverty, dilapidated homes
Miserable jobs, miserable wages
We have nothing to live for

Sire
How ever can any human live

Within
The Ruins of Despair?

Sire, I humbly ask you;
How can we live
When there are
Conceited Bastards
Who have the luxury of
Analysing the intricate values
Of the square root of
Minus zero multiplies
By the inverse ratios
Of zero
In their abstract mathematics
Studies

While we, here, have no education, Sire
Our jaded children's books
Have books whose papers crumble
As they desperately try to read
Crumbs of information
That was meant to elevate them from their
Revolting poverty

You have humans shaking
Their corpulent bodies
Across the wonderful distances of this exotic earth

While we, here, Sire
Live, to breathe
So, in time, we may
Painfully suffocate
And die

What, then is your message?
Living by bread alone is not enough?
Really?
How exactly do you like to see us live, Sire?

🙰

How Come No One Noticed the Killers of Jesus?

He spoke of love
Breathed, dreamed love
Infused and
Exuded Love
Loved all of us and also
For Humanity and her evil ways;
Lord Jesus; butchered in the
Name of the Love of the Kiss
Of Hypocrisy -
The Hypocrisy
That Man finds
So natural

Gentle soul!
Betrayed by the Greatest of your Followers
Betrayed by them, that so adored and
Them, that so night and day venerated
You the most
Betrayed by them, those whose
Worshipped you day and night

Strange imprints!
Did you people notice?
Imprints were deliberately
Planted everywhere and in front of our paths that we
Daily trod upon
How was it we did not understand and feel
What venality was silently mumbling against us
Silently, but with dead seriousness in their intentions
To execute their plans of butchery

And who were these creators of psychotic malevolence
Creators of clues and imprints and
Suggestive seductive whispers?
Do you not stop to think
In your materialistic, phony, plastic,
Under nourishing lives that it was none other
Than them, the same adoring crowds?
Yes, they were, after all, the same venerable
The Founding Brothers and Sisters
Who were your determined killers
Of Him that they
Night and day

Venerated
As a Spokesman for our Lord God

It was themselves, you knew and talked to
Who so casually replaced the truths
With the simplest and most digestible sugary falsities
And why did not your Disciples
Seriously notice these clues of the evil intentions
That were so abruptly to be
His sickening Reality
Committed with such real love
Against our and Your Beloved Son?

I declared to no one
Out there
In my imagined audience
My presumed people
You see

Endless deaths
Are coming
Now
Through the reels of our news
And nothing was ever surviving
The bloody blasts from the merrily drunken revolutionaries
Who are killing now
For killing's sake
And so let's laugh out this unending holocaust night
Out

No one really understands this
System that we once create in our ancient past
Listen, here!
A charming serial killer
Philosophised about the differing values
Of existence
And in the end
Yes, he
Managed to don the ugly and deformed clown's killer mask
And entertain all you approving fools
Out there
you did laugh
And enjoy
This squalid situation

ᏮᏮ

How Many Times Do You Feel Empty?

Beauty child
Abandoned
Repeatedly
By fathers
Mothers and lovers
What more can be
For you?
How many times do you feel
Being just nowhere
In rich conversations
That eventually make no sense
How many times
Do you love
Pointlessly
You laugh
And then think
Why am I laughing
Nothing is funny actually
That lunch of hypocrisies
Distasteful evenings of perpetually hidden yawning
Jig sawed life
Fragmenting gradually
In my hatreds and deep slumber
Tell me now
Of all your reminisces and lies
Yes, I was there
Did you forget
Bastard fool
I was there
When you wept
At the funeral
Of my Dad
That you so hated
Beautiful Daughter
Beginning to smile
Didn't you know
Who I am?
I am your Daddy
Eternal
Baby girl
I'm going to be yours forever.

꧅

How Will You Judge Yourself in Your Final Days?

You lived in so many disguises
You laughed so many smiles
You cried so many emotions;
They that were
To you
Mixtures of
Heavenly tears
And heavenly hatreds;
And,
Now you are
Nothing
Just a dreaded emptiness
Emptied of all your disguises, smiles
Emotions and tears of all hues;
There you appear now
Sitting pointlessly
At this finality
Facing you immediately
Wherein God has brought you
Face to face with your mortality!
You the silliest tramp
And you the mightiest King
Sit now together
Hand in hand trembling
In this court of Judgement;
Idiots!
Too late now!
What mattered in your lives
Was your ethics
And not your zeal;
What, then, did you understand?
So, say to me
You who understood nothing,
For what is the value of one human
If he or she
Is a murderer
Sir and Madam?
Think

Though, yes it be too late
Think
What is your value to God
If you have
Unethically hurt the suffering
Souls?
What words affected you
In your lives
When in truth, you
Were driven by evil
When, you were driven by bastards?
Or did you really think
You were driven by saints?
Did you live, work, behave, act, love, rule
Lawfully
Or unlawfully?
Or perhaps,
To you -
You never even cared for the difference
Between the two?

ဆင

Howls of an Insane Woman

1. A vague impression wept
Dews of insecure passion
Small passions founded on severe fear
Unheard of

2. Another beauty dies
Here and now
As we think and as we read now
Another dying suffering one
Suffocates now
From another grotesque grasp
Of Humanity

3. And these ones will not fade away
Their corners coming closer
As their sorrows exponentially expand
So weep no more
My face dries
For none can actually hear us here

4. O vague impressions!
The wilderness and loneliness
Is our home
Our forced home
Unheard and unseen personalities
We are, we think
Do you really think you can fly anywhere?

5. A staggering heart once wrote poetry
Unguided words
Words from a fragmented, severely
Sliced up heart
An unknowing heart
Did you scream at the sorrows you daily see
The hardships you daily suffer
The opportunities weep
Savoir! Saviour!
Save our lives!
Here and now

6. This meaninglessness is killing us all!
I scream!
Far too profoundly

Here is our now and our today
This is our 'now'
Not tomorrow
And not our yesterdays
It's our 'Now's' that we need
You saviours out there!

7. There was Hunger and a hating Smile
Youth turned away wearily
The candles of love wept
Melting breaths
A scream rings in me
With no hope of escape
A beauty
Whose life parallels my life

8. Suffering
Believing she has convictions
But she never really knew herself
But the screams reverberated endlessly
While the babies
Of my mind shrieked.

⣿⣿

Human Clashes

The painful
Lecture
By the wounded
Ones
Is being neglected
All across
Unbelievable sceneries
Of carnage
Where humans
Become
As ants
And gangrene's logic
Wins over
Our freedom.

ତ୍ତ

Humanity's Proud Achievements

When sickness is coughing into your Self
You see
These antagonistic spirits within you
Undefined, indefinable
Killing each other
Abstract hatreds
Grand monuments that happily testify
To Man's cruelty
And useless blood-letting
Slaves are dying
And barons are smiling
Within this congested world
Within which exist billions of
Exposed ideas and dying humans
Packed in tiny heated cages
Bleeding from pain
Squashed humans
Burning sweat
No water, killing thirst
While soldiers ape history's heroes
And die in a splash of grotesque tragedies
Wealthy pirates must also die
While more criminals are calculating
In their splendid palaces
What to do next
This is their privilege, no?
You are weak
While they are standing there
Fooling you
Their images and shadows fooling you

෨෬

Humanity's Vomit has Been Discussed Before

Changing your lies again, as you think that you must do
Yesterday they were an indefinable blue red blur
Weren't they?
The liars of saintly Truth!
Blasting hearts of men, women, children and babies
And they are taken to some overcrowded, dirty hospitals
With no professional staffs at all
Suddenly and you're in a mad rushing flow of screams, beginning and
Incomprehensible pleas
Death is facing your living senses now
Staring at you intently now
Operating and digging ugly brittle needles inside you as they joke and gossip out loud
Your heart is being physically ripped apart
By these laughing 'doctors'
Listen to the abandoned soldier of emptiness
Walking for a million miles all in a perpetual, imposed daze
With no fourth hand raincoat
In this insulting weather
Blinded by strictly enforced unfairness
Another tears is forced out
From the shrivelled mummified corpses
My God! When will we ever see the helping hand again?
When?
Another invisible victim, another ghostly tear
Another this
Another that
And all humanity's vomit has been talked about and tasted and analyzed.

☙❧

Humans are Hurtful Crumbs

Hopeful last breaths
Death's final instincts
Receding from you;
When will we accept
The meek have gone?
When will we eye the final mountaintop?

Truths weeping, as the end nears
As honesty lies crippled, beaten and bruised beyond repair
And the pulverized human dust can no longer speak
How can we ever
Allow ourselves to be so abused?

Tell me, then of your spiritually desolate sighs
Tell me, of the horrors minute by minute
How will I stand on that day
As my life on your earth dies of grief wrenching?

For the Humiliated
For the Degraded
For the Ashamed
You
In context, understand your enemies
In context, measure the moments foul
The days foul
Measure the Contexts of Grief
The ills that occur may be your doings.

Others are unjust, I know
But try to understand that 'justice' is abstract:
I tell you sincerely,
Humans do not feel justice
And so justice is meaningless.

Understand humans because
By understanding them
You then know what to do;
Understand the worthlessness of your Savage Species
Understand that humans are mostly
Hurtful Crumbs from the Devil's faeces;
Only then will you seek fulfilment
And, also comprehension
Of what your Life is.

 හ

Humans Hopeful, Though Wrecked

Truths sail away
Unto waters troubled
Humans hopeful, though wrecked
Distances deemed too far
Expanses unyielding
A Christ solitary walks
Himself hung
And death become freedom
Planet Earth – strange you are!
Why so much of your paths
Lie so tortured?

🙚🙘

Hypocrite: Don't You Feel Yet?

Oh! You actors to spare minutes and grins
Complex confusions to mask
In hideous laughter so lewd and loud
Turn so inward and admit folly's price
So ruining a style to exist
Withering all strengths from so within
So daily in persistence
Forever so flamboyant and decaying;
Raise an arm – feel it now
Does it still stand to be yours?
Or so you claim...
Your convictions in unmarked graveyards
Row after row...
After a row
And for what use be they?
Those whose roots so entangle one another
A smile to forge –
Or so circumstances seem upon your
And for what, in your final, ultimate end?
Or for whom?
Oh! A soul so decentralized, unfocused in truth
In a quiet civil war so unassumed
Admit a thousand shades of will – all so true
And don't you know
In this one your life
Your eagle eyes glare weakness
To this soulless world you deem so smooth?
Oh! And how!
And how grief-filled and confused emptiness
Stare out upon this scriptless, leaderless play of life
Quick! Tear a smile, lest humans know...
And so, inward drained and bleeding
Out-ward joyous and alive
Ancient contrasts –
Between Magnificence and Depravity
Filled so many pages of History before...
Good-night.

☙❧

I am a Failure

Let me here write
Over myself
Body and Mind
In this uncared for place
A unity
Has been fragmented
And now lost
I am walking nowhere
In my mistakes
I wrote wrong truths
In their times
I thought they were True
But these selfsame 'Truths' and You tore me away
From God
You tore me away
So far from
My wandering worthy life
And now I am homeless
Here
In this new life
Where I so fluently reside
In self-bitterness
Within so much beauty
Surrounding me
I know
I just fail successfully
Unable to reach
Unable to achieve
Purity of mind
This was, after all
Only my beginning
So imagine the rest!
And for me
It was such a sickening horror
As I drowned in my own
Quiet self-hating inner contemplation
Of a pathetic life
That can only glow
And plough on still
With another
Dirty drink or more.

ᘒ

I am a Sickening Life

What can one word
Express
What can one heart
Feel
Game over!
If everyone
Sees lies all around
Strange realities
Vague visions
Infinite pain
In deep
Within me
Unending
Deep
Within my frail structure
Killing depression
Through anger
I am being here
Existing
You're all so far away
And our union
May heal me
Though these are uncertain thoughts
Sickening life
I am a sickening life

&

I am People, Destructive and Inspiring

People are questions
The future of remorse
In a show of vague, undefined motions
That explained what needs to be done
If Humanity is to succeed
In reaching Happiness
And yet
Look!
Yawning winks
Tempting or disgusting
Telling me
Of the flamboyant hollowness in your thinking
You are indeed the 'People'
Destructive and inspiring
Across wretched lands and starved tombs.

ஒஏ

I Know I'm Killing Myself

I try here
This life
To restart
Bread
I dream of
That warm bed
I need
But is not mine
And I turn away
From them all
Because within me
Is an unknown disease
Naturally enough
It betrays my sanity

This beautiful food here
That is not for me
I stand here and nowhere
Unaware of the dangers
The mistakes I do
Are piling up
And these years of mine
Are telling me
That my trials of tearful
Pain
Will eventually
Murder my soul.

৪৩

I Need You Now St. Mary Magdalene

And what, now, woman?
What now do you think?
What now can we discuss?
Was it madness that spoke to you?
You jeered at what you screamed were
The joys of crucifixions
Magdalene!
Daughter of an unknown village
Did you come to save me?
Or what else were your intentions, then?
I was, I am, I will
Always be a Failure
No matter who I am
So maybe you ought to turn away
Yes, you who may have to look now
At my face
There's my inscription
There my epitaph for everyone
Why am I faithless and angry, you gently ask me?
Why?
You do not understand me
Well, you don't need to.

☙❧

I Tried to Explain to Her

Myself
I tried to refresh her Mind
To the Inexactitudes of Beauty's Truth
Wherein she then found me even more
Loathsome

You see, listen, here:
She tended to readily
Sway towards the jesters
Made of rosy perfume

I complained!
But to what avail?
None!
I began to think elsewhere
What if my 'words' have no
Connectivity
To this Damsel?
Then what ought I to do?

Her Mind told her Whispers
That were
In essence
I can confirm
Rather far too confusing
Romantic language?
What absurdities!
And so, indeed
She became confused
As I
Tried to express my opinion on what is going on
Between us
Which was precisely that which
Is inexact
But her Heart drove her fanatically
Towards Irrationality
Whereby that really
All over again
Did leave me
All too Disconnected
From her

One dull night

She screamed, "So what then do you say love is after all?"
I exclaimed calmly,
"What love is, "
She interrupted me, screaming further,
"Speak words, you make no sense!
"Always, when you speak, I lose myself
"And that does frighten me"

And, I attempted to paint for her a candid portrait
Of what 'love' is and
What 'love' is not
She did not like the portrait at all
As per the usual
"Ah well", I said, sighing
"For this is after all, is what love is
"Never! never!" she screamed
Typically

I told her:
"You do remind me of Dorian Gray!
"Do you not?

"For you deny reality
"Of the indefinables
"You do not understand
"That nothing is Certain
"In our Existence
"Save the dour End!
"And that is where
"You find so many
"Difficulties
"In your fully perturbed
"Solitary life".

ᘓᘒ

If an Empty Bowl or Plate Appeals for Itself

If an empty bowl or plate appeals for itself
Appeals for food
If a moment cries songs
Needing sustenance
And all they get
Are songs
That revolve dizzily
Vomitingly
And if a dubious hand shaking
Aches for meaningful humanity's touch
And if a smile tells you a sincere lie
And if a curse teaches you to hope for tomorrow
Where will you then stand
With whom
Culture of stupidity
Culture of brain damaging
Silliness
Culture of apathy
Culture needing boredom
And culture feeding from boredom
And some sing words of meanings
Some speak words of relevance
Yet curtains rise and the actors so often see an empty applauding audience
Your culture is draining people's sanity
These are the truths and their consequences.

ക്ക

Incest Victim –

excuse the facts. they lie to themselves.
standing lonely and alone. as i stood there crying.
tears of rain. windswept and unheard.
aghast child. speaking tones of suffering.
where were your childhood plans. in your hours safe?
as the angry ones gloat. as the hungry ones weep. as i saw the many.
in their hours dictated. i need a game puzzling.
heralding a time of supremacy. speaking of times unparalleled.
untying your soul.
nothing is existence. and existence is nothing.
sorrow is a smile. and your smiles are a crucifix.
painted and merged on your faces. everywhere.
people seeking avenues and paths.
money. your problem. rent your problem. friendships your problem.
affairs your problem. fear your problems dragging you inside.
and nowhere. we do not know ourselves. i am saying.
in ourselves. nothingness.
do we know.
nothing. do we care.
nothing. do we paint.
nothing. do we behave.
nothing do we feel.
nothing do we care.
admit and lie then.
admit and lie.

ల్ఞ

Ignorant Innocence

Greetings, tender girls!
Flowers
Reflecting your unknown futures;
Greetings!
Sweet smiles
How little you may seem
Against the truths that will
Confront you
All
Darlings of life!
Today
Remember
That truth will catch up with you;
No matter
How ignorant
You may ever be.

৩৫

Is This Love and Life?

Illuminated sinister thoughts
But why?
You say, he says, they saw, we heard
But where were they all?
A heavy liberal torch you sought to triumph for
And a torch that will cost you what, you never thought to ask?

Love: that mystery so bothersome, fickle and indefinable
Diverting our severely earnest gazes from
The tearing creativity of the isolated genius
And selfish, idiotic Humanity, no less breaks into sexual giggles
While I see within and outside
Victims torn, shred, shrivelled asunder randomly, rapidly, lovingly

Laws of love drill craters in the brains of
The humans whose innocence is unmatched by any depth of stupidity
See them, will you?
See the languid rows of emaciated, fracturing humans
In the crowds that are bestial creatures fallible, anxious and insecure
And Oh!
How they
Fill so much thoughts, brimming over
Humans and their humanity!
What a miserable, repugnant sticky paradox
That so creates those selfish threads
Of a conspicuous feeling of vapid venality

Tearful; in your venomous convictions
Yet discarding the weeping's and pleas of beautiful brothers?
Oh no, this is not my love!
Never my sweet destiny
Never...
For I stand firm
To declare forever:
Stake me!
Rather than seek this
Crippling living

ᘓᘓ

Is This Our Life?

Pass by the groaning graves
Stillness now
What once was a furious party
Lives of splendour & decadence
Now lie solemnly dead
Think of your mind
Think of your emotions
Think of your thoughts
Where have they been?
And so think where they now stand
The severely sad
Are struggling to cope
Fearing suicide
And yet
Fearing life itself
What a planet
What a world
Beauties
Cripples
Listening to me
Where is it all
Your civilization
Where can it be
I wonder
When we listen
To nothing
And no one
In our rage
What are the 'rules' for this, your life?
What are the 'guidelines'?
Is anyone there to tell me?
Or are we born naked here
And are we to live without reason
Where are the blessed ones?
Where are the loving ones?
Where are the compassionate ones?
Where are the faithful ones?
I'm searching still
Seeking to disentangle myself
From this filth
From myself
From this disconnected life

છક

It's Not for You

When leaves may dry
When hurt is anxious
And when is a devil
Please, then;
Answer my words -
Sweet distant mother!
Answer my needs!

When lovers are thrown out
Just as the hungry are
Abandoned
And when the living see
No more hope
What, then, would you speak, my lovers?

When the burned ones
Feel nothing but hatred
Racing out through their pulses
My beloved ones;
The salvation may be near
But nowhere near to you
At all.

&

It's Over

If I write
My words make sense
Fractured brain
Smashed teeth
Rippcd tongue
You knew that
You knew what you do against yourself
But your conscience
Begs to differ
So
I became a professional Hater
Of your Mankind
You who speak what pleases lips
You who practice saying 'Thank You'
And hourly butchery
Against idiots
That I and we are
When I laugh I see
The Spit of Satan
When you practice your 'Welcomes'
My mind's skin shudders
I see rapists of children
Defilers and smiling
For when you chose to release Barabbas
You thereby crucified humanity
I too lost my sanity then
You slice testicles like carvers do
Unto admiring crowds
How can it all be so?
I've asked myself before
But, now, no more.

ೞ

I've Tattooed Your Soul on My Blood

Christ how much
You smell
Glorious
And when you sleep
It is eternal spirituality
Puppy..
I die as I live
Next to you
Baby boy
So far apart we are
And yet we sleep so close
Izzet
I die for you
I've tattooed your soul on my blood
And now I can only wait for you
To love me

෨෬

Judas' Last Passion Letter to Jesus

The windy evening
Threatens the moment
To end
A candle's
Sorrowful life.

Degraded Martyr
Begging the Hungry
To feel their Soul's Heaven
While the Meek behind you
Yawn
At your last words.

My Father!
All truths can be
Seemingly never-ending
In beautiful expanses
Forever and beyond.

Accidents from a mistake
Ends my Epic life
So, I'll bid a Sincere farewell now
To all passion's lies.

Ancient Victim!
Still writing tender scripts
For feuding lovers?
I tell you
The Poor
Will always forsake you.

Soon I shall cease to be
Forever and beyond in a Deathly ending
Betwixt the Silence and the Symphony
Of my mem'ries' moments.

My God!
My God!
I shall
Meet you!

For I was Acting
My favourite friends
I knew not what I did
So now, beg and reason with *Me*
And for my compassion's love and mercy.

My Remorse
For the Forsaken Child
Is screaming through
His Tears
On this Ending
Night.

ღ

Killer Clown That Fooled You

I lovingly spoke of love
To Humanity and her evil ways
You people who tell me
You were constantly being
Betrayed by the greatest of lovers
Strange imprints from your lives
That you couldn't analyse
Planted everywhere
By happy killers
So I sincerely and diligently replaced the truths
With the simplest and most digestible falsities
Oh what a performance!
What a spectacular show!

Out there we were
Through time
My real and imagined audiences
Presumed to know yourselves
You see
Death will come
As a surprise to you all
Though the reels of our news
Can be compared to your lives
Nothing ever really survives in your memory
The bloody blasts from the merrily drunken Revolutionaries
Who are killing now
For killing's sake
And so join in
And let's laugh out this unending holocaust Night!

No one really understands this
System that we once created
In our ancient past
The Political system
The Economic system
Listen, here
A charming serial killer
Philosophised about the differing colours
Of existence
And in the end
Yes, he
Managed to don the clown's Killer mask
And entertain all you wildly approving fools
Out there
You did laugh
And enjoy
This squalid situation
Didn't you
And now you lecture unto me
The differing colours of morality?

෧෧

Killing an Innocent Bird

You try now
To speak, as you paint
This emotion
That turns nowhere
Because
No one
Understands idiotic artists
And trying here
To be real
In your eyes of funereal coldness
Endless grave
Morrison's grave
You walk through
They all point ahead
And tell their path
This path
That end
To a certain beginning
Then you find the
Immaculate Woman
That has announced her
Sudden Virginity

Hopeless child
Dying tonight
Nowhere to be felt
Lapsing within
And into reality
Through these words
Of fractured intentions and meanings

Child of my memory
My first boy
What crime did I commit
Inside you
As this passion
Flies inside
So deep
My mind
I ring and dial
All these piano bars
Just as I ring and dial
On my brain

And his words come out here
Scarring you perhaps
Killing me
And no communication
Is there

Did I go beyond the truth
Sweet mother
Dying in her grief
No one here
Will listen
So die
Then
Alone

☙❧

Lady of the Secluded Ponds

Eyeless flower
In minds of unrest
Sing this melody in warmth abundant.

Troubled Skies have chosen
To forsake you
While you crowds seek to intermingle
With lovers un-affected
Do you yet again fail to comprehend?

Moon-less sky
Come and perchance you may
Yearn in me, to visualise
A show of Truth
That dances
The Dance of Closure

And yes what cried – cried!
That is my understanding
Of History
Where outbreaks of madness
Virulently burst out
Far too often
In uncontrollable rages;

Gentle lady!
In the midst of it all;
Come to feel
That your
Flowers in your mouth
Will bring bitterness
And not deliverance
For that which is
Constitutionally brittle
Cannot last

Think, then
Think!
Soft Lady
Of Ponds Warmly
Enclosed.

ଛଔ

Last Letter of a Convicted Man

What can I think anymore
The Sum of my life?
My worth?
My memories, children and other thoughts like that -
The roar has ended!
And my
Dust has decided to settle down.

Judgement, verdict have been pronounced against me
Again and again.
So, for now the question is of acceptance
That an end
Is truly nigh bound.

Silly sad fool
Did I really think
I was going to make it
Over and above what my steely stupidities
Defined my truths to be?

❦

Letter Found on Dead Woman

O Sweetness
And if life
So now
Still fails me
I guess
I'll so surrender then
To this
My lost
Smile
And her only hurt secret
That so affected my grief

This, then
Was my beginning
In a world, my world
Of such an expanding sorrow

And so Goodnight
Sweetness
Of my
Own life
That forever allowed me
Her serious pleasures
Whist so denying me
Clearness of Mind
Goodnight.

৪৯

Life is a Series of Lies Till You Die

Beginning the day in life
Where pompous psychologists routinely speak of
A love
Hidden and hurt;
Psychologist who need to see other sarcastic psychologists
To Talk about a
An insincere Poet's suicide
Who couldn't express his 'Love'
In those odd circumstances?
And so ended it all.
Really?

Angels weeping again; hear, see their gazes of utter disbelief
At our repeated stupidities
As all of you drink
To socialise
Your needs
Feeding an absence
And filling the hole
Of your brains
Yearning for coherence
Or, do you call it 'unity'?

You are living a lie
Life is a series of lies till you die!

Your embarrassed laughter, gets you nowhere
Your nervousness, uncertainty and fearing your own mind
Gets you nowhere
And the Tensions, insecurities and not knowing how to behave in public
Is still getting you nowhere;
So, you continue walking on
In this sick, meandering path;
Well, listen if you do listen
This path means
Life will kill dreadfully and determinedly;
And you may see, if you contemplate -

Your slow end rolling, heaving towards your uncertain Self
The pangs of the bitterest failures, the failures that have left you
In stinging pain and indescribable panic
And the humiliating pointless moments of euphoria
So drink!
Because, you must to diffuse feared thoughts
All of you, are a plasma mass of undefined Needs
Why do you call for figureheads?
So you can love them, weep for them
Clothe your insecurities with them;

But I say – if you seek to listen,
They are but
Idiot idols, manufactured from fake flowing shadows, they are
Reflecting the anguished fear within your Self.

တင

Letter From a Madman

A scream
In my memory
I heard abstractly
While you talked to me
All I needed were humans
Who chose to be Real
How will it be
When I come to say my 'Farewells' to you?
Towns you built are architecturally horrific
Humane Expressiveness denied repeatedly
A madman spoke words none heard
Turned his brush strokes inside
Inner meanings to be meant unto whom?
He spoke of love and deprivations unendurable
Killing his bearings and balance
Christened himself as sour emptiness
How sad must you become?
Can you understand, readers years from now?
Strangers coldened by life's clicks and pixels
Wrote ambitious manuscripts and then duly discarded them
The needy, wet oceans profound demanded succour from the madman
Whose inner cadaver remained languishing there
Devoured by existing dry fish
Within the those breathless layers of stingy darknesses
Waters of no oxygen and light
Where terrified fish strove to survive, though in pain
Where did humanity meaningfully touch with this chapter in Nature's history?
I never understood
Madman journeyed 'Neath the heavens black and starless
The ocean's bed invited me there
Because that's where I belong
I guess?

ଚେ

Life of the Impossible

1. I hear you
Sad of the Earth
The Sadness
Everywhere
I notice you all
The fear, trapped by solid isolation
Can you save your Selves?
The anxious, running ones
Can you save yours Selves?
The lonely, shamed ones
Can save your Selves?
The crushed, breathless ones
Can you save your Selves?
No, no, you cannot.
Save your Selves
For this Life
Is by far too, too
Strict in its unscrupulous laws

2. I see the abandoned child
And the wounded ones
Suffering again tonight
And will be the same tomorrow
Sad of The Earth!
Are Weeping
Again today
Tonight
What kind of Life is this?
I say!
Is this Life?
Or is this the Death of Man?
I ask you
To ask yourselves
Don't you ever come to notice
The broken masses
Of suffering Humans
All around this dying planet?

3. The sorrows of Man
And of the Sorrows
Of Mankind and the
Sorrows of Humanity
Cry out again and again

In a planet of the Unhearing
Read me well: I never said the 'Deaf'
I say the 'Unhearing'
How much more sorrow can Man
Endure?

4.   In a planet of arrogant Masters
Who decide whatever they want
From us
They choose to do as they wish
And you have no Say
You are not allowed one Emotion
To save yourself
From this wretched Life of Poverty in a Rich Land

5.   Life of Difficulties!
From this repulsive Life, wherein you the powerful ones
So casually
Dismiss us, regarding us as Nothing
Which, if truth were to be said, we are
Really
We are Nothing in this,
Which is entirely your world

৩৫

Life's Concrete Knowledge

Some spoke, some cried, some threatened lives by words
A dawn's dawning yawning gradually for hope
Progress unsure...the crowds threatened to know
To bleed and to ulcerate for crumbs of words
Blinding and to thrust waves ferocious
Onto souls drowning and insecure by life's concrete
Knowledge that was stabbed by wealth
Shaken by demons of luxury and rotten frontiers
Twisted by unemotional, greedy creatures unalive
Crowds burning just to feel, to rage, to burst
To tear open these wings
To thunder passions across the Heavens ripped so meekly apart
Crowds so expecting the fire...the crowning, triumphing speeches
Expecting the grand gestures, artistic and fulsome
Fulminating towards kings parasitical and stuffed vermin
Guillotined labour drenched rivers and oceans
To scream forth and to be alive in haste.

ভৎ

Lily Say "Goodnight"

O the Love
O the Love we have known
And the Tears
And the Tears pride has masked
'Cross a heart
And into an art

O the Age
O the Age we suspend
And in Times
And in Times we suspend
An innocence
For a life to beg an end

So say "Goodnight"

All your life

Lily say "Goodbye"

O the Deaths
O the Deaths we have known
And the Times
And the Times we have thrown
All to waste thrown
And our hearts were never grown

O the Wind
O the Wind across the seas
And the Eye
And the eyeless child we feel
'Cross the years
And into our Fears

So say "Goodnight"

All your life

Lily say "Goodbye"

ᚖᚖ

Listen to Me: Stubborn Recluse

You stand, rigid, frigid
In this
One-sided truth
That only you see

Quietly sad
You stand
Frigid, rigid, unable to bend
Or relax
In that selfish decrepit eye of yours
That causes you so much
Angry hurt
And you do not question
Wherefrom,
Wherefrom did all my
Maladies
Originate?

You may think you see
These mixtures
Of vulgar and pleasing moments
That pass
You by
Years ago;

You still
Stubbornly insist that
You will only see
From that cornered
Eyeball of yours
That is so self-centered –

So, why, oh God, why do you believe
In those demonic demons
That fester within
Your entirely brittle physicality?

Why do you
'Believe'
These 'realities' to be
'Truths' for you and for everyone else?

A thriving child
You were
Once
Pleasant, cuddly, edible and adorable to nibble at!
Yes, I remember you

And for now
Wrinkles are entrenched deeper
Within your fast fading 'beauty';
As you slowly, surely pass out
In this earth
You mistook for
A hell –

Listen, Man;
I shall now
Speak to you straight;
My truth
Begs your
Truth
And so
I say to you:

To release this bird
Caged in your mind;
And let one half,
Meet the other
Half:

For you can't live otherwise,
And you can't try otherwise,
Even though, yes you still stand alone, stubborn and
Determined!
In your putrefied truth
You are fading
From yourself
And you do not even realize that

You say to me:
"Release this bird
And let one half
Meet the other half
What, for God's sakes, do you mean?"

I tell you
Come to be
Accepting the hated contradictions
In your soul and mind
And allow them not
To fight anymore;
For so long you thought 'Unity of Mind'
Meant there shall be no contradictions
You remained wretchedly wrong
And I tell you now,
Let contradictions
Exist mutually within your mind
And allow
Discipline to unite them!

You observe expressions of laughter
That we manufacture for the pleasant night
Yes, these are called superficialities
And, I may add the word,
Idiotic superficialities!

So you feel some lightness, unburdened;
But listen to my voice:
You will still remain alone
Returning to a home
No one knew of
And now
Now even the light
Is waving goodbye to you!
Doesn't it seem
They all are waving
Goodbye to you?
Doesn't it all seem
They all are waving farewell to you?

Listen, soul;
It is yourself
That is
Waving that farewell
To your self
While we stand and watch
So change
Away from your stubborn ways
And only then can
You live within
The pleasures
Produced by lush and exuberant
Freedom!

లిం

Listen to Me – I'm the Madman

Feeling feelings
That come from nowhere
Sinking my life
While my
Surfaces are barely reaching
Their stable mind

Soulful fright
Sparkles that dazzle, yes, but have no meaning
For myself
Go within
In my mind's shredded images
That you call vision
But that are for my fractured Self
Incoherent and blurred

I feel only
Smiles of Sickness
Bare teeth of inconceivable stench
Exposing inner frailty
That just turns out
To be my own
Pulsating fear

I guess
I try
Trying to be
What I know
And what I know not
Trying to think
I think
I am
A fright
To you
And myself

Swaying sceneries
Make me dizzy
Yes!
The same sceneries
You people
That you people
Call your

Daily life
Some shine, and some not really
And if you are interested to understand
For my mind
And its Self
The results are fear
And meaningless
All over again
For me

My Tears provoke
You
But, why?
You say,
I'm paranoid?
You fools!

Who exactly are the persons
Do you think
That is, if you think
Look at my finger and where and at whom it is pointing
Again, I scream to you sane citizens
What are their identities?
Of those and of them that are today and now
Holding all the thickest drenched sickening ropes
Meant for our fractured
Necks and Brains
Again and again?

When do you think
You may cease
This paralysing pressure?
That you apply
Upon me
Stabbing me?
Piercing?
Slicing?
Hurting?
Me
All
Within
My turmoil

Vomit is spinning
In my mind
Leave them –

Yes, them!
They are the Christ's that are weeping
Hysterically
Moving me
Beyond sanity
While, where are you all?

And your polite rules are
Moving me
Way way far too much
For my stability
Polite subhumans
Flying
Make me
Flying
Make me
Flying from you all
From you all
Let me make me - fly far from you all!

Harrowing
Humans
Listen calmly
To my mind
Listen
To your own
Screams shrieks and all the rest
Before you think to presume to judge
Because you too
Some day
May suddenly
Come to be
Plunging in
My world!

ॐ

Lives of Distressing Anarchy

Tell the children aching for meaning
The tremors frightening
The work numbing in their eyes blurred, shrivelled
Where starvations are the polite norm
No one else could dictate the times
In the hopes passing by and receding beyond reach
I spoke of sceneries mosaic
Unbroken somehow
Where the times appealed unto us for serious change
Where meanings sincere searched for our whereabouts
Where prisoners of war pleaded for our consciousness cosmic
Where ragged children dying cried tears that were bleeding blood
Save our flooded homes and lives
The sun cries for the twilight of the evening
You must have understood the images you felt
Or were your hopes also drowned by the manic floods within our minds?
And you were seriously regarded as beautiful?
What minds did speak to you?
And what did your upbringing mean to you
And what did your education mean to you
What do you recall from your past
Not much, I know
Remember the butchered ones!
Remember the sorrowful ones!
Crying quietly and unheard still
The night beckons us to a liberating death
A death that will unite us all
Nothing will matter
Because only
The criminals and the illiterate judges matter
On this earth.

∽

Living in a Wilderness

I see my eyes
Reverting
Bulging inwards
Yet, speaking outside
Of shrill fears

Feeling hues and nuances indefinable
Lovely contrasts
Jagged emotions,
Acres of mutilated humans
Serrated teeth
Severing carotid veins
Jugular explosions
Blood frothing inside
Mine mind
That throws itself
Weeping far too low
On this strangled ground
Near my skin

Far too many times
I've felt, seen, experienced blazing humiliations
Searing slicing fear
That I can never ever
Describe to you
And so
I'm writing for no one
I know

Listen to these skeletal notes
Being played out
Manic piano loving my drunken guitar
Producing acoustic screams
Hurling within
My hatreds
That need to prop my reason of d'être

Isn't that language
Being expressed
Spouted out
Created forth frothing from these experiences
That are harrowing?

ʘʘ

Lonely Telephone

City teenagers hurling about within their lives
Absurd places to live in, I feel
Consequences never being understood
And so, mindless action and devastating hurt ensues again
And times are uncaring
Didn't you know?
Walls bare, barren and sweating frightening you
But why?
Pay shall be low!
So it was decreed
By smirking legislators light years
Away from us
So bleed on;
Your brain is unaware
Friends fade soon
Opportunities sinister and momentary wanted you
Lonely telephone
That you gaze at
In your gloomy, wet room
Irrelevant information piles up within
Recognizable faces mean little to you
Glamorous personalities all conform
Times are repetitive and cliché-like
Humans!
Growing older so soon?
Days monotone continue passing by
And so your life styles remain intact.

&C.

Longing to Break Free

Sweet truth
Living this life
Now
Your anger
Turns still
In a time
When Mankind just forgot you
And you forgot Mankind
As we all walk
In life
Ignoring each other
And needing each other
So sad
Is this path of life
You humans
Just walk
Looking at each other
In fear
And yet
Longing to break free!

ಶಿ

Madness of Life Itself

To feed, to relate
On Humanity, and its presumed worthiness
Is such a daunting task, I should know;
To ask and seek hearts bleeding and
That are proud that are so severely burdened
Is unbearable

Under the toiling sun that scatters its loving, naive fruits
Unknown slaves are burying waves and burying ripples of emotions of seething hatreds
Screaming and seeking invisible alleys of freedom
Never to grip their master's merciless madness
That he defined as 'integrity'

While wearied babies are unable to listen anymore to this consistent, persisting babble
Turning and weeping in such severe black sorrow at this Trial of Life seemingly eternal
While none can sense, nor relate to these virulently sickening times
Motions, cries and edicts casually swaying in order to grind down the goodness of labour
Piercing and tormenting and taunting the hapless and the crushed ones
The millions yearning for an ending final to satisfy justice
Their cries of tears are spraying this disgraceful globe
Still all unheard, unfelt it seems
Chained, locked, fettered, murdered children
And drunken princes glibly vomiting their happiness away
There exists neither sense nor just beauty to care for
Nor any serious nation to care for anymore
Nor any ideology, nor party
For all are
Actors
Politicians, Psychiatrists, Businessmen, Friends
They're all
Actors
Dancing in their narcissistic centre of pathological lies

No more sane thoughts to feed credibility can be found
Corpses of virile and depraved sensuality are in their gatherings in drunken taverns of shallowness
Where you see endless examinations seeking sane beauty from greasy vice

৪৩

Madness of Mind

Salty feast for the thirsty
Torturers, seething livid
Struggling to contain their base infamy
Hungry ravenous bestial eyes
Rotating, smiling grotesquely
At their prey
Wingless birds
The nightmare is pressuring you in its
Intensities and in its
Variations of mental horror
And perpetual stalking fear
Shaking control, gradually losing self control
Blurring vision
Colours far too strong for me
Everything is against me
Piercing me
Sweating inside my gushing mind
Your palpitating heart reminding you
Of your present, endless situation, dragging on
Beyond all reason,
I cannot reason with madness
Madness is frantic
Pointlessly running against my security
Gushing out within my holes
Ever more viscous, jelly black fear
The feast, recall
Never ends
The images and depths of fear deepen in an abyss
I cannot talk about or think of
In the ugliness of madness in all its
Intensities

I know
I am victimized
How can I get out of this
Filthy hole?
Where are the maps?
The guidelines?
For this wicked civilization
That has left us
Stranded
In surreally insane no man lands?
Frustrating conversations that I must make
And listen to
Endless boring laughter that I must make
And experience
Pointless days that I must go through daily
Inherently ugly jobs I must breathe
I'm speaking too much
As I fall within my struggling, dissolving Self.

ॐ

Man at Odds With Himself

A belief that comes
To die
In its earliest hour
Creating an unexpected sorrow;

And, in its post-mortem trial
The Philosophy of Mind
Exists
To argue against itself.

This, then, has been your Decay
A word, so simple
In your heart
You live
Within the death
Of Faith and Belief

My friend!
How Bitter separation is
We all know
Especially from oneself.

&oe;

Memories of a Childhood

Eyes surrendering
To a ravaging snow
Scenes expansive
Amidst decaying conversations
Suddenly
Times and their moments
Erode feelings
And erase minds.

Lover from afar!
Uncaring I feel
Lovers
Of skins sagging
And happiness withering
Away
In silent anger
Trying to express
The memory of hurt
Because of scenes
So ravaging

Mental Patient Writing

I love you all you
Or, all of you
I guess
I should write
Properly

Happy ones
Yes you!
Living you all
Drinking air
Vacuous nonentities
Am I describing myself or you?

Supreme in my brutal
Powerlessness
Inertia is my magnificent pulse
Loss is my definition
That defines
My dumbest elemental stench

I live to see so-called teeth grinding
My teeth
Actually
I talk about
Am I being grammatical correct for you all?

Worms satanic
Within
Eyeballs melting from Sorrow
And they then
Continually
Keep
Bleeding and looking fractured and pale
Didn't Sane People
Tell me
Eyes are Souls into
Our lost Selves?
Or, something similar?

Weeping Nerves
That are
To dry
To move
Without a breakdown
I am scared, in a bed, a room
I involuntarily break my idiotically stretched lips
So, I become shy
From you all onlookers
Doctors and Visitors
Or Relatives?
Who's who here?

And,
If I fake
That pointless
Smile
For any ashamed passerby
A sad banner
Shall be there –
Announcing my
Smashed structure
And functionless music
Don't you ever get it?
The Madman's Grammar is different from your Grammar
But that shouldn't confuse you too much

Will you now inform my homeless address
Of my abandoned Mind and Flesh.

Moments of Life

Traumas of children so fierce to be
Come, love for one moment and see
What 'Sanity' has instructed you to do
My lovers my friends
What 'Sanity' has come to be, in our sordid times
See their tattered, bludgeoned eyes
Oceanic scales of turmoil
Hear the squeaky cries of the young ones
Ones stabbed by far too much hunger
And others stabbed by sorrows so simple
O! See what Sanity's come to be!
My friends;
Come see the simple Meaning of History
So Unjoyous and tragic a tale
These are Moments of Life...

Yes, these are Moments of Life...

Whispered threatening words and feelings, you hear and sense in your unprotected skin
Can't believe the shades of Reality that can be so gruesome
And so I am suspecting so many people of self-muting themselves
Unable to come to terms
With accidents unforeseen to seem
Unable to believe this is real
Unable to believe that, yes, these are the Moments of our Lives.

The haunted shrivelling children look still at you
They tell you so repeatedly, with their voices now croaking
Their Maturity's Cloak has been
Blown so ferociously
By murderer's fanatical determination to inflict needless tortures
And still, you stand wherever you may be
Refusing to believe
Refusing to understand that 'mercy' is a Man-made fabrication
To lure the innocent one's to the butcher's juicy hacking knives
So, let us try to awaken our Soul's
To the Reality of Life
And its most repulsive Moments.

☙❧

Moon-Like Landscapes Before You

Trails of honesty
Yearnings over highways deep
Where forests shrieked of their yesteryears
Their livid vines questioning
Questions futile really
For we never were able to understand their antique language

I see depths of innocence
Out in places moon-like
In their instructive barrenness
Where goodness is trampled all over again
While all my ears hear
Were solemn sermons were mass delivered for money
And all I heard
Were atheist priests who joyfully whistled meaningless tunes alone

Darling child
Darling molested tot
Where are you this night
The manic woman batterer who thundered out a speech yesterday
A speech on why we must desist from sarcasm
A speech on the need for austerity
A speech on self-denial

What can I be?
What can I exist as?
Here in such a world of theatre?
How much can I and should I feel?
How real should I be?
Where can I ever find the questionable answers?
Where?
I heard of a picture perfect paradise somewhere
I heard of a community communal
But the rains pour once more
But my dreams faded due to my savaging circumstances
I don't know how much more
How much longer
Can I go on?

For, I can scream no more
With a throat such as I have now
A world can be beautiful?
A paradise can be here on earth?
They say to me such thoughts
I no longer know or feel
Much, anymore
But I do believe
That we are here on earth
To experience hell in its proper elements
And from that context
We must learn wisdom for our
Hereafter.

ՏՁ

Murderer's Repentance

Sudden Truth
Of a forgotten
Tomb
Returns

Killing his
Eye's Hatred;

So forgive them
Then
Just as they
Themselves
Dare to
Cry

In a truth
Of self-honesty.

৪৫

My Baby Boy, Pidi

Sweet son
My beautiful baby boy!
My angel baby
I see enemies supporting you
Their kisses are stabs
Their love is poison
Screaming to discard you
Beautiful boy
Pidi!
Understand my attempts
To gather truths
From a stolen basket of mainly stupidities
And when I lie down
I see angels
In my bed
And while I survive
I live through the Devil's mercy
How odd!
How odd!
I adopted two gorgeous girls
And I did love them
In eternity
But they were not able
To realize
My thoughts
For them
At all.

৪৩

My Beloved Son

Sweet child
And if I did regret my life
Will you understand
These mistakes
And endless errors
Coming over me
Beloved son
Forgive me
My faults
For I have not sinned
In this life.

❦

My Death

Winding down
Nowhere
On a crowded London road
Sinking or drowning
Loud joyful conversations amidst chic clothes
Everywhere see contrasts between
The happy and the desperate humans
Their Hands are tied
As they seek to beg
While others live within mouths already stuffed
Criminals screaming songs righteous
Down my smoky congested lungs
Their bulging inquisitive lurid eyeballs
Questioning their needing lusts
The furious stench
Is heavy acidic, heavy alcoholic
As they seek my votes, my money and my home
Historical buildings, monuments and stones weeping uncontrollably
For they always feel they're being ignored
Panic stricken minds tearing themselves and their flesh shred by shred
Is it sane
This truth
Of life?
Can it be
Sane to feel 'unreal'?
To see, to experience
Your mind being outside your skull's nerves?
Bastard thoughts daily, in and out, and daily in your skin
Crushing your hopeful functions
Creating in me
Dead spirits, crushed spirits, ending severely now
And ultimately surrendering
I'm so hoping to be near you
So soon
That's one meagre consolation
I'll soon hope to hear that adored celestial music
I burn with that ardent need
For so long
But not for long anymore.

৪৩

My Endless False Truths

I am
Trying
To be
A moment of joy
Trying
To believe
My love
Is ebbing
I am
Going nowhere
I realize
I am dying in my
Endless false truths

๑๑

My Exit That I Couldn't Find

And yes, if my life
Was so to be
An ending dilemma
That I couldn't
Solve
Then shouldn't I be looking for
An Exit for myself?

Gentle souls
Listen to my emotions
Just as I then again
Tried to escape and fail

My own
Heartbreaking rain
This that pours
And seethes
So continually
Upon my invisible raw Mind
Leaving me unable to push on and ahead

This I can't understand;
My Exit
Unto Happiness
I could never find -
Therein was my
Simple Sorrow.

My Favourite Firing Squad

Fire at me now
And let's get it over with
After all
Didn't I remind you
Enough times
That
You are
And
You were
My favourite firing squad?

ഇൗ

My Psychotic Fires

I've been through
Psychotic fires
Going through my hated sensitivities
Dad I didn't expect you to die
It was just too sudden for me
You did wrong
Many wrongs
Sir
But your death murdered me
What happened to you
In just a few days
You became a dying man
You were whoring and gambling
And then
A few days later
You were ordered to quietly die
On an unconcerned random bed
Casually Stuffed
With tubes
By our best
Illiterate 'nurses'
My Dad
You were dying
Surrounded by the dregs
And pits
Of 'humans'
And what could I do?

ॐ

My Recurring Nightmare

Shifty Lovers
Glamorous Murderers and shy psychiatrists
Unsure of their own texts
Liars trying to be genuine
Hoping we'll donate more of our love and spirit
And directionless criticizers
Interacting mindlessly
In order to exploit us

Sinful eyes leering
Seeking passionately to destroy unfocused minds
Just as unworldly slick aristocrats
Smash wonderfully expensive old wines
In their hollow dust barren palaces
Within their dim-witted bobbing skulls
Thinking Glitz produces Serenity

And the peasant bland looking virgin who spoke in an expressionist language
Whose exquisiteness surpasses breathtaking palaces of grandeur and majesty
Sadly though,
She Suffers from inexplicable mounting pains in her touched Flesh
Her lurid revelations and garishly explicit forethoughts
Have been premeditatedly
Diminished by her self-imposed juicy veil

Beg from these gruesome, ghastly beggars
Begging for morsels of sanity from the least qualified
This is our only living
In our unblessed
Native land!

These discontented orphans squealed
As charming languid prostitutes yawn their stench out
Preparing themselves, as they must
For the serious hours of the night of labour

Our Prophets are
Unceremoniously being butchered
There beyond our lazy eyes
And I can never understand
You paedophiles!
Who roam and rule our bewildering earth
How, then, I think
Is this civilisation so gushingly accepting of you?
Can I tell myself 'Goodnight' now, please?
From this sickening nightmare
Of nightmares
That visits me every Night?

∽∾

Navigating the Waves of Our Life

We live through the arduous waves
That our society and the streets throw at us
You try to sense the directions they're coming from
Giving, trying to laugh, and hoping therefrom to find out where to duck and journey on
And then, when hurt slams you
Pierces you
Severely
You feel you cannot be still
You're trembling
You feel you're losing your physicality
People define you as a bland entity
Of nothing whatsoever
No letters of yours remind you of anything meaningful
No love of yours is vivid anymore
Despair
Creates
Your challenged identities
You are laughing
At our turbulence
Is that right?
You think:
"Well, these are my personal experiences
"I did die so many times
"In one breath
"Just as I pronounced
"Myself to be definitely decent and mildly insane."

But others judged and saw you as a traitor
So who's judgement ought to prevail here?
In Life's unbalanced paths
I ask you
Woman
We are speeding on with our so-called 'living',
And to do so, we must all be Lying for and
Against each another
And perhaps so much more seriously
We're convincing ourselves of our fabrications
That in their turn
Will define your identity
And dictate to you how to act and react
In your daily life

Dear souls
Dear dying ones
Should you know *Not* your own selves
Then how do you
Navigate through these waves of your
Life then?

৩৩

No Escape From PANIC

I think
I am losing my soul
My mind
Past people have died
Looking at me
From their desecrated graves
Blinded by blackness taking over my sight
Turmoil threatening
My time-consuming pleasantries
While random others
Surrounding me
Laugh pleasantly
I fear heights
Now imagine
Some body
Is trying to throw me out
From an airplane
I'm terrified
But actually I'm at home
It's 3.00 in the morning
My five year old
Is sleeping next to me

What can I do?
Where can I go?
What medicine can I take?
Nothing, of course
Because this is January, 2003
And our technology *has No* effective
Medicine as yet
So I must suffer
And it's not really suffering
Really
It's so much more and beyond
Such fear I can never describe
Passionate hysterical fear
Fear that is out of control
Fear that consumes you
There is no G.O.D. at that moment
Nothing
No one
Nothing
Except your Fear
Playing with You.

&&

No One Can Love You as I do, Dear Son

And who will be there
Just for you
You think?
See me
See that your thoughts, hurt and bleeding feelings
Don't go really too far out there
Will they?
Think, Son, think,
As you may well fade out
Fading out from your self
For if you think just what
I am talking about
Words I did use for you
In my corrupted life
I sincerely described to you
As Hell incarnate
But I still try to tell you
Sweet Grace
No one can help you
No one
Like I can
Gentle Son
No one
So learn
Learn from me
Your Eternal Daddy

ᚖᚕ

Ocean and Soul

From the darkest depths
We hear murmurs
Ah! What laws govern here?
What rules do apply?
Murmurs mysterious and so vague
Bursting forth from a withering soul
Oh you! Trembling and alone
What do you fear?
What is it that so pierces you?
Prayers from the depths of your soul
Reaching out for a charitable soul.

Oh strange seas!
Mysterious and so compromising
You are ever changeful
Your soul has little unity
Your depths see little that is understood
Oh strange seas!
Remember your greatest companion
He is the wretched one
Whom none likes
And none understands
For, he too, strange seas
He too is dark and mysterious
Wild and passionate
Unknown and feared
Despised and hated
Hounded and oh so pierced.

What makes you tremble –
Fool?
What makes you rage –
Ocean?
What is encompassed within you –
Soul?
Mighty ocean?
Ah! Sometimes your vision is
Crystal-like
And sometimes you see but dancing shadows
Ah Ocean and Soul
What strange lovers indeed!

৪৩

Old Man Thinking

Your Letters
Your expressions
Changing smiles
Facing me
I no longer recognise you
Or anyone
For that
Is my truth

You are all
Plastic within raging fire
Though you never let
What was stolen from me
To be returned
I guess it
Was hard for you to give up
That which was never yours

But in the end
I was faced with a totality
Of nothing
And so
I surrendered to you all

When truth is
Eviscerated
Piece by piece
And love is
Mangled
Fiercely
By smiling
Happily
Condescending
Powerful people
What can you do?
Who
Is it
That is there
Tapping inside your minds?

What?
You there -
I ask;

I am still seeking hope
Just before
I too may well give up
Because this life
May well have been
Created for the kings
And the torturers
Only.
How can I know?
What I can never know?
And you idiots are still asking me
About unknowable's?

Did I think of them that rule you and I –
Yes, them
The Gamblers who seriously
Believed in the chances of their wisdom
And forgot their obsessions?
Of course, I did!
I guess, that was my obsession!
What else could I think of?

Because life
Is one hate filled
Chance filled
Moment after another
Moment of the
Bill of no rights
For the undersclasses;

Do you feel
With me?
There is no
Love
I tell you!
There are no friends!
Even though
You may see
A Christ gives unto thee
His milk
Do not over-interpret that searing moment
For it will not be of any value
In your daily life for bread
And security

You laugh, you sneer at others
I ask why?
You say:
"My circumstances created
That which is what constitutes me
Can you deny that?"
No I cannot, I replied
But I tell you
You can change
You say:
"How can I and you, two sad atoms, change this vile earth?"
And, yes I agree.

☾☽

Our Odyssey

Stifling minds and grease-laden wretchedness to behold
In this meandering Odyssey we gather the fruits of warnings
Laden with sorrowful histories
Weeping Woman! As a journey we are destined and predetermined
This *appea*l is for our Unity to transverse all trials
So shed weaknesses and adore all mightiness!
East and West *may* be so irreconcilable
And brothers *may* still neglect each other
We my Friend shall outlast them all
In our Odyssey pure and brave
In this Dangerous and Surreal Reality...

ॐ

On Death Row

Killing life
That ever tries to live
That is I
Anyone behaving
I'm killing!
Don't you ever forget me
Just before
I may die!

৩৫

Panic Attacks are Fun

(You Should Try Them)

A waterless feast for the thirsty
Torturers
Struggling to restrain their base Infamy
Hungry ravenous bestial eyes
Smiling grotesquely
At their Prey
Wingless birds
The nightmare is still swirling in its
Intensity
Variations of horror
And perpetual stalking fear
Shaking eyeballs
Blurring visions
Colours far too strong
Piercing
Sweating inside
Palpitating heart
Driest mouth
Piercing
Beyond any reason
Pointlessly running
From the excessively, maniacal seething Fear
Never ending

The deformed visions deepen
Yet disconnecting themselves
From my shaking Self
Withering my 'I'
I see a threatening ugliness staring at me
I know
I am victimized
How can I get out of this?
Filthy stench of a greasy pit
Where are the maps?
The guidelines?
Where are the physicians?
Promoting this vicious
Civilization
That I do swear
Is even sicker than I am
For you have left us all
Stranded
Surrounded
In a surreally insane No Man's Land

ౚ

Panic Feeling

I think
I lose my soul
My mind
Past people have died
Looking at me
From their desecrated graves
Blinded by blackness
Turmoil threatening
My pleasantries
While others
Surrounding me
Laugh pleasantly
I fear heights
Now imagine
Some body
Wishes to throw me out
From an airplane
I'm terrified
But actually I'm at home
It's 3 in the morning
My five year old
Is sleeping next to me
What can I do?
Where can I go?
What medicine can I take?
Nothing, of course
Because this is January 2003
And our technology has no effective
Medicine as yet
So I suffer
And it's not really suffering
Really
It's so much more and beyond
Such fear I can never describe
Passionate hysterical fear
Fear that is out of control
Fear that consumes you
There is no GOD at that moment
Nothing
No one

Panic

You can tremble
In these here
This final
Unknown twist
In your life where
An avalanche of fear
Is zooming on you
With a certainty fearful.

Your confused eyes
Feeling that pain
Again
Furiously interacting
Within and outside
Frightening yourself
So deep
Back
Into your solitary
Self of helplessness.

Unable to understand
Any longer
The hatreds fuming
In your life
And
Occupying your
Living spirit
To death.

ॐ

Passion Play

Location: Desert Shore, Bitterly Cold Night, next to strong waves from the ocean.
Characters: Man ((M) and his Lover, a Woman (W).

W: "Search as I forever do, in manifold ways unknown, I seek but to love thee, and the meagre goodness from Life, with steely ardour - my armour faithful."

M: "Alone I may be, and still, yes I love thee; these days heavy are and beset I am by burdensome trivialities, but I remain trusting, though my corner so narrow remain."

W: "My Love! Your speech I hear aloud and thine lips I live within and yet, my Love, all Solitude I am. Man! I am unaided! In this journey of sinful thorns, my love, in this unforgiving journey, this blurred odyssey, I stand alone".

M: "This trial you speak of, but I do know of it well; so, listen then: within the strength of trusted togetherness we can plough on, though everlasting harm shall do its spiteful tricks, warm to our united truth shall we remain."

W: *(Surprised)* "O! My love! This thought I cannot hear! My life, my destiny, is but mine. And all have their own solitary roads of jagged rocks to embrace, like it we or not. We heartbreaking earthly sad beasts, either fiercely clutch at integrity, or we do let it go to perish away."

M: *(Confused)* "My Love! I do hear, I do hear. But when Times decide on burdening us, what then can we achieve? To face Reality within the frail arms of solitude is to ignore, to refuse the severe threats of repulsive grins."

(Silence)

M: *(Passionately)* "O! My sweet! Only in us, can we envelope, through joined, clasped warmth can we be as one united! The screams that so truly are meant to slice us off, only we, our Unity, can destroy. For mine eyes can only find sleep in your ears, and it is so - for otherwise nothing and no one can be."

W: *(Angry)* "My Passion too is bubbling for thine bewildered ears. Am I not your soul? Do we not suffer as one? Do we not reflect as one? Am I not your lover true? Is not our warmth not weighty to our fickle bones?"

(Silence)

W: *(Passionate)* "But, Lover, this much ought I to formally declare unto thee: For our eyes, and all eyes, envision *unequally* at one another. Till eternity, in its casual, indifferent flicker, snatches at us all wretched mortals, the gazes from lords to paupers remain veritably mismatched. O my passion! My woeful heart! These words I thunder forth defines love unfeigned, and what mine eyes do pour out unto thine ears is authenticity true.

(Silence)

W: *(Passionately)* "*What joined mem'ries you choose to caress may possess thee, but your exactness for what love is to you, doth not dwell in mine mind. What tears, what weepings you do, fall stormily upon thine own soul's wildernesses.* You choose to be chained by changing visions and indefinite sentiments of light weight – though so poignant at the moment they veritably are?"

M: *(Inquiring)* "My love! I cherish thee; where hast thou been in thine mind, for now ye talk of that truth you relate to in your heart. Your pronouncements, what depths I do feel! Can it perchance be that my passion has strayed our winds far from me?"

W: "No, my love! Why is anger, I feel, lush on thine tongue?"

M: *(Surprised and Frightened)* "Anger! I am too distant from that affliction! But yes, I feel my words make only for unstable murmurs in my breath."

W: *(Quietly)* "Then, do tell me, lover, who do your murmurs betray - myself or yourself then?"

M: *(Quietly)* "Perhaps so, perhaps so. But my anxiety wilfully demands of me to eradicate your vision."

W: *(Firmly)* "You answer naught from my undemanding question. Or, are mine meanings too violent for you? What aches thee?"

M: *(Passionately)* "My sweet! In so many moments, I created mysterious planets for thee! Bizarre worlds of contrasts and opposites and musical words of antiquity and sensual ravines. My love! I, my soul, my life, my inner deepest breath, tempted as I am by Fates' inscrutable cruelties to ashamedly yield, I have yet always expressed to mine eyes' heart, though they be in bleak darkness, to faithfully fight without pause all shades of vice and still yet - with loving integrity; I have stood with arms of righteousness and love for thee up and never down! Yes, sincere good and venal ill remain joined in life for all to feel, but you knew it was not for me to disentangle them. And so, I pronounce unto thee, still, and yet ever and ever more, my love for thee, though still beholding a thousand mountains before me, I remain sturdy for thee; I remain undisturbed by burly laws, and by exotic dictums, I stand fierce and unhurt, save in your absence."

W: *(With Sadness)* "My beloved, your vivid voice stabs the falsehoods for thee, and I say unto thee, unto thee your excessive and unreasonable chains, and for myself my unreasonable and extreme chains remain."

M: *(Shocked)* "But I burden thee with no steely chains, nor verbal fetters! For naught I produce for thee save grace, passion and freedom to love for us both to be in Unity Sacred! Dost thou embrace my visions as 'shackles', then 'tis better we agree to class that which we are as but madness! Hear me, for my tears now must truly change their colours!"

W: *(Determined)* "Your feverish hands clutch only upon mine erratic wings!"

M: *(Anger)* "Never! Never! For I clutch only to destroy all malevolence; as for thee, Lady of the purest, untouched, guarded, secluded Ponds, I seek to unshackle for you the scattered, scared shadows that yearn for thine sovereignty. And what is this 'sovereignty' but our Sacred Union? What curse deemest you I impose? Do you equal my purest passions with atrocities? Murmur unto mine ears, your clearest love for me."

W: "Ah! You enquire of me my 'sincerity' for thee? What demands!"

(Silence)

M: "I see naught but heaving forests of love betwixt us, and yet, you discover my words being 'demanding'?"

W: *(Drily)* "Perchance, your visions are indistinct and ever more blurred, through these years cannot be ignored."

M: *(Begging)* "My love! All mine life, though it be lengthy, I fought most venal tyranny, and for this moment, you question my righteousness?"

W: *(Indignantly)* "I have been plunged into seas hostile and I have plunged in a thousand miles of inert minds troubled beyond conceivable comprehension and I have yet to have my Right for my own greedy, ravenous flesh to be vigorously and forcefully embraced by sensuality and serenity. Yes, I do love thee, and yet in our union, as in all unions, I have been adorned with naught, save snickering, gossiping scenes of festive balls, games, chatter and farewells, themselves festooned within silly and sincerely stupid smiles and frowns, and shallow tears and never ending ludicrous chatter unworthy of monkeys conversing. I have met programmed rows of pats, respect and all other so-called decent intents and gestures, but, where, lover that you are of mine, where does my personal heart, throb and manically vibrate, save in your heavenly imaginations?"

(Silence)

W: *(Quietly but Determinedly)* "My love! I truly thee love and with passions, I tell you, of proportions of precise exactitudes; in your eyes I have witnessed symphonies of exquisiteness; and, I of thee ask: where dwelleth your own love for myself in thine body?"

(Silence)

W: *(Passionate)* "Do you recognise the changing structures that form this, that I name 'My Love'? In my solitude eternal, I do evermore and always do pause, and be pensive, and be thinking of questions, such as 'where', 'why', 'when' 'how', and 'which' should be my path; I am forever and ever more searching, seeking the heavens of every corner, and the irritable tempests, within my changing self as they themselves do try to seek me, and we forever, through inconceivable murkiness, do try to assemble the everlasting entirety of these disorganized puzzles into some measure of comprehensible cohesion that 'I' am. That is how the 'I' you love is forever changing and thereby formulating itself, and within all these meandering passions, and endless errors, where am I to feel thee? Where? And where do you seek me? In which land? In which forest? You trivialise my beingness as you focus upon my lands as being that which so effortless to find, and yet, you are much too distant from an understanding of my conflicting, emerging civilisations."

(Silence)

W: *(Passionate)* If the utterance 'Never' is pathetic for thee, then allow me to introduce you to my latest heart: for it screams out that single, protracted utterance! *Never!* My love, these winds of raging wraths, both within and outside by flesh, must and can only be annihilated by mine own sincerities – were I not to play against my own self. My uncontrolled desires and, yes, thirsty manic passions can only be tempered and thoroughly satiated to the utter brim, by mine own loving, sources of pleasure, my own uncontrollable ecstasies. As for the rest of bodily pleasures, my own erroneous words, speeches and utterances can only be severed and sliced by my tranquillity."

M: (Resigned) "I hear thine words. Do not abandon me.
Do not destroy our civilisation of justice."

W: "What we share, the bonds, are enjoyment. Listen though to mine lips: enjoyment is what - when it is to be compared with convulsive ecstatic quivers of satisfaction?"

M: *(Puzzled)* "And what of all our journeys to attain that unity? For all that, is it to be of mere insignificance? And if that be your truth, for what then did we toil and labour for unity of minds and bodies?"

W: *(Laughing)* "Did you understand from Life itself, that here it was, grandly to proclaim its furtive faces unto thine own awaiting face?! "

M: *(Baffled)* "It was so far too plain and vastly clear unto me these sceneries we faced before our loving bodies."

W: "Yes, and I too, did see them with thee. Our four eyes, did see unity for that flicker of time. How true you speak! But, time clocked on, I saw you as you stood there, moving nowhere, unawares that it was your duty to squash onwards whatever vile breaths faced us."

M: *(Desperate)* "And did I not? Did I abandon thee in these crushing paths?"

W: *(Accusing)* "No, you did not. Never, once did you abandon me. I ask of thee; for what sense do we feel a need for a continuation of these gruelling marches? For unity? For love? Or, is love unity? Was that and is this our reason for us to carry on with these shackles?"

M: "For assuredly, yes, and more yes, I tell thee! Toil and gruelling dawns, and unbearable evenings and the whitest of nights are all for the sacred attainment of that heavenly summit of joy I name as blessed 'Love'."

W: *(Assured)* "And, Sire, what if my nerves, blood and bodily hunger tell thee in truth that we, all of us, need no longer, and need never in truth, to undertake these paths, for we find naught that nourishes us at the blessed summit of your definition of what 'Love' is?"

M: *(Confused & Sad)* "So, I falter here and now upon understanding your speech; do I reason from thee that our loving days in unity are frivolously bygone now?"

W: *(Calmly & Gracefully)* "Do the wandering birds, and do the blind bats, and do the reckless storms, and do the blindly, raging waves and do the supremely arrogant oceans eternally march on in but one direction only with the savage passage of time within their particular lives? You did pronounce that you built planets for our unity; well then, did you not view how planets endlessly revolve along the same path?"

(Pause)

W: *(Calmly & with Dignity)* "For, Sire, I am not as a Planet - could you not feel that throughout our journeys? *You endlessly query and question 'who' it is that 'I' am? Well, I speak this much on myself; I am as the birds, and the bats, and the storms and the waves and the oceans.*"

M: *(Angry)* "Woman! I can only then tell of thee that you are naught but feuding clutter and violent disarray!"

W: *(Unconcerned)* "Those are your words. Not mine. Speak for what you wish, Sire."

M: *(Angry)* "And I stand here, before thee, in anger – nay, more, more! In fury!"

W: *(Laughing)* "For what? For the deeds that created but sticky, and grimy grains of sand for the undoubted pleasure our eyes?"

M: "And so you label our truths, our love so much! Fair indeed, you speak, Woman of Justice."

W: *(Arrogantly)* "*Man! Express your delights for your own delights. And, alas, there the circle and reality ends – and it ends only for you.* That is one morsel of truth for you to ponder. What we 'created' and what we 'loved' was never and never, ever be the same for you as it is for me. Are you a sincere believer that your personal vision is the same sight all other seeing creatures envision?"

M: *(Angry)* "Woman, you enrage me! Your arrogance is drenching thine rags."

W: *(Sarcastic)* "'Tis the Man with no reason who allows his breath and words to be a veritable cesspool of fuming stenches!"

M: "But I, that I am, no longer can define your contours?"

W: *(Pointedly)* "Precisely, Man, precisely. Perhaps, now you have come closer to the vulnerable shores of reality!"

M: *(Confused)* "Do you express that you are ever varying and so for that reason there is not a one unified you?"

W: *(Calmly)* "For we are all 'varying', to borrow your word – if you do so allow me, Sire. *There was never 'unity' of soul, nor mind, nor self, nor of any one personality. This, I desire, that you may understand.*"

M: *(Aghast)* "Then if that be your truth and then, are we naught but multitudes of ever changing confusions, Lady of the Desert?"

W: (Calmly) "Yes and no! For those who are muscular and full of fertile vigour in their flesh, and in their intellects, and those that are severely and strictly scholastic, then they do need and they can succeed in time, in their never ending struggle to bring together the mutually antagonistic factions of that which constitutes our beingness. And, as for the dense brained soulless beings, then, it is equally veritably true that, a descent into madness can be rapidly produced, since from their erratic constituents, they cannot attract together these antagonistic and mutually-hating emotions in some vision of cohesion, and thus mayhem can be fashioned."

(Silence)

M: (Calmly) "So, pray do tell me, where does Love and Justice and Truth and Morality stand in your universe?"

W: (Serenely) "That has been mine desire to hear the words being produced from your lips, Man!"

(Pause)

W: "So, now perhaps, your sight may be getting clearer, for your question is certainly apt. Foremost, we pathetic mortals, we the be are forever slimy specks of sand that crumbles, must necessarily seek to survive and flourish within whatever forest, desert, meadow we find ourselves cast upon."

M: (Startled) "At what cost, Woman? At the expense of Morality?"

W: (Rapidly) "Yes and no."

M: (Shocked) "Horrendous! How can you spout out such filth?"

W: (Quietly) "Restrain your stupidities, and give more room to your intelligence, Sire."

(Silence)

W: (Gracefully) "In times of trouble, what can Man do when he be forced to embrace evil, even though he finds the act of the embrace loathsome, but he does what he does for the truth of his vital existence to continue. Only when he need never embrace vile, and then allows himself to commit the act, then he is for certainty to incur the everlasting wrath of God. Evil is thus never one truth to be utterly rejected, perchance you may now see. "

M: (Calm but Tired) "I follow your words and their ideas therein."

W: (Gracefully) "When you talk to me on Man and everlasting, conflicting changes within that self-same creature, I tell you with all the earnestness that I possess, of what God has scattered and endowed upon me; for this beast, we all call in unity Man, this creature has far too many a numberless number of mutually self-contradicting, distrusting, loving, hating, inspiring and a never ending number of feelings and emotions that are in constant flow and change – as in any rapid river descending unto its eventual destination, which in its case, is the sea, while in our case, it is Death itself for sure."

M: (Despair) "And how can this beast 'love' anyone within this welter of confusion?"

W: *(Rapidly)* "He cannot!"

M: *(Rapidly, Begging)* "But Man and Woman do love with bristling passions! Do you deny that, Woman?!"

W: *(Calmly, eyes downwards looking)* "Yes, and no. Since the beast has needs, based on his vastly intricate constituents, to 'love' his fellow beast, he imagines and believes in his imagination that he is really in a situation of 'love' and that – as you put it, is 'bristling with passion'."

M: *(Softly)* "So, Woman, it all but *illusions*, you speak?"

W: *(Sorrowfully)* "Yes, and no. I tell you that as far the 'loving' beast, since he genuinely believes that this is 'love', then it truly becomes 'love' for him. But, as far as the wider truth of reality expresses itself in its manifold manners, we sadly know that he is nowhere near 'love' and that he is being but his mere self – which is to say, being typically delusional!"

M: *(Exasperated)* "My Lord! *Everything for you is "yes and no"*; you are yourself nothing but energy that is contradictory. I mean to ask you, as per my last question - is Man in love or is he not in love and yet, before me, here, I see you produce yet ever more paradoxically senseless answers! Have you nothing that lies purely straight before thine eyes and mind?"

W: *(Impatient)* "Alas, you Man, if your mind is not as endowed as it may need to be, then the fault is surely not to be mine, is it? That is a question for you to ask our dear God upon your particular meeting with Him."

M: *(Angry)* "Are you daring to speak that I am daft, you foolish Woman?"

W: *(Amused)* "Precisely. Well, actually not precisely. Far more than 'daft'."

M: *(Sarcastic)* "Anyone who does not agree with you is dim?"

W: *(Laughing sarcastically)* "Man, what a senseless fool you indeed are. I never have spoken words that anyone who is in 'disagreement' with me must be dim. However, and this sentence is certainly for you: I do say that if Man is incapable of understanding my words, then he must be not dissimilar to our cousins, the apes."

M: *(Pleading)* "Woman! I ask you, can Love be - or can it not be?"

W: *(Subdued)* "Permit me, Man, how do you explain unto me what 'Love' is?"

M: *(In anger and pride)* "What is Love? You ask that of me? I, a warrior all my decades, fighting furiously and fighting passionately against all oppressors, against all evil-doers, and you say to me what is 'Love'?"

W: *(Inquisitive)* "You have expressed to me that you have fought all your brief life against injustice, and that is noble by all standards. But where is it that I am meant to witness you finding this Love of thine?"

M: "Love is the struggle itself against tyranny itself, do you happen to see naught but veils and mists and fogs?"

W: *(Sarcastic)* "So, if I choose to fight against tyrannical
rulers, then I produce 'Love' from my actions?"

M: *(Frantic)* "If you choose to fight the tyrannical ruler for the single purpose of removing
that vile ruler in the hope of liberating the people of land, then, that is one form of love
indeed. Then there is the other kind of love, Woman, which I *desperately, terribly* seek you
to understand my mind. For, Woman, when Lover seeks to fight tyranny in order for the
purpose of liberating his particular Love of his life, then that, I tell you in all earnestness
then that too is also a noble form and sacred type of Love. Do you find my words sensible?"

W: *(Bored)* "And, pray, if you wish to please my sensibility, how does your Lover
know that he *knows* his Lover? Wherefrom does he get that *certainty*?"

M: *(Excited & Speaking Rapidly)* "He has that knowledge from Love itself! *The energy
of Love itself informs the Lover who to 'love' – and what he or she must do in order to achieve
union with the chosen opposite lover.* You see how blessed and powerful Love is for us
mere mortals? It is an *intelligent form of energy*, Lady, think of my words. How do atoms
know where to go and what to do? They just 'know'. Maybe, 'tis God that tells them.
Here too, I speak to you, perchance God directs this exemplary 'Energy' called Love, to
inform Lover to approach his or her Lover and that is why they fight injustice, sacrifice,
and bleed tears of blood, till they truly one day, some day, join in flesh and mind!"

W: "And what of the changes that Man and Woman do undergo –
how does Lover continue to relate to his or her opposite?"

M: "Again, for your beautiful question, I tell you this: *only* for the Lover who has been
blessed with Love from our Lord Himself, then, no matter what changes exist within
his opposite, the Lover will still, and for eternity love his Woman! That is the meaning
of Love, Woman! You ask me, what is the definition of Love? I answer you truly, that
is the meaning: that I, your Lover, will fight liars, and jesters, and hypocrites, and
cruel deceivers for Your Sacred Cause and – hear me here – and even if you should die,
the Man who loves, will fight still and forever even after your expiration! Never, ever
to capitulate! Do you feel the boiling energy of furious rage that will not and never,
ever accept the rule of the hypocrites and oppressors who oppressed my Lover?"

W: "What is your meaning of 'Sacred Cause'?"

M: "You missed a crucial vital, life producing word: 'Your'."

W: *(Puzzled)* "'Your' - And what?"

M: "Woman of Endless Beauties! *The Sacred Cause can mean nothing when in the absence
of the word 'Your'.* So, listen now: the Lover will fight unto brutal, painful death, *only
for Your* Sacred Cause. That Sacred Cause is for your Lover to do for eternity to fight
for *your, and only for* your dignity, and only for your liberation, and only for your
freedom, and only for your joy, and only for your prosperity, and only for your joy. The
'Sacred Cause' speaks to me who the Lovers love. And 'Your Sacred Cause' means

your Lover will fight forever in order to give unto you and only you, your joy, your mirth, your pleasure, your comfort and all the beauties of our miserable existence."

W: (Bored) "But why take unto your already sun-drenched,
parched and burdened body all these arduous tasks?"

M: (Surprised) "What? You still do not comprehend nor words,
nor ideas and nothing for all that matters?!"

W: "No, unto *you* is to be an answer that needs be forthcoming. Speak
for me, why should we beasts undertake all these blood-drenched
battles and all for the attainment of the 'Love' of a Woman?"

M: "For sure! Indeed! That is a the beauty and reality and the truth of Love, for just
as Life itself a never ending life and death struggle for existence, so too, is then,
Love, for to attain Love, Man and Woman, or 'beasts' as you choose to call us, must
necessarily and seek to ceaselessly struggle against death, and gloom, and despair
to possess that holy union between flesh and mind between Man and Woman."

(Silence)

M: "To me, I believe that you feel Union is not that so necessary for Man and Woman?"

W: (Surprised) "On the precise opposite! Union is a need of all beasts, for it
is a fundamental instinct within our starving bosoms. But your definition
of what that 'Union' is meant to be, differs from your vision."

(Silence)

W: "Love is the Union of mind and flesh. That we all agree upon."

M: "Indeed."

W: "But in my planet, beasts, Man and Woman, ever *change* in their visions and in
their feelings and in their needs and in their appetites and in their desires so that
what Man originally 'loved' is no longer the same Woman that he once did love.
And so how can you 'love' that which has utterly and completely altered into another
being. That is truly a contradiction that defines nonsense; so, now – what say you?"

M: (Baffled): "Well, even though we do change with time, experiences and events
and the effects of powerful memories, real Love will simply overcome all these
difficulties and soon Flesh will reroute its way back to its Lover's Flesh and Mind
will re-unite with his Lover's Mind. And should the two humans fail to reunite
then all that can be said is that it was never Sacred Love in the first place."

W: "Yes, Man, but why crucify yourself for that Union? Union
can be achieved through much easier means and paths."

M: (Shocked) "Why do you underrate the power of the eternal Union?"

W: (Laughing) "I've answered you already, dear Man. For what you so call 'Love' and

'Sacred' and 'Union' are all true to me – *but they can all be achieved by much simpler ways than from your tortuous journeys* – and you describe the struggle to achieve Union of flesh and mind as being like a life and death struggle. Well, listen to me, ye mortal Man, for you have overburdened yourself when I assuredly tell you, there are easier paths."

(Pause)

W: "Maybe not as intense, pleasure-wise, as your struggles, but as for the truth that God has allowed us only a brief moment in life wherein we are breathing, I can say this much: it is much better to follow the path I have chosen."

M: "But did you not before, unto may speak, telling me that your path for the Sacred Union of Flesh and Mind was exceedingly more pleasurable?"

W: "Conversing is the need to be as the tide. I can tell you this much: pleasure and its ferocious, unyielding intensities can only be experienced and defined by the receiver and so – unto you I say, perchance yours are weightier than mine."

M: "And so now what, Fair Lady?"

W: "And for now, either dream on or think on - in the paths you shall have to necessarily endure."

M: "And then?"

W: "Senseless questions requires of me none to be replied to."

M: *(Confused)* "I ask thee, do we be on this fiery planet, for the sake of sufferance only?"

W: "Yes, and no. I tell you that what is 'north' is unto thee, is true. Is it not. You see 'north' is the direction that only you and your constituents see, and, perhaps we ought to all applaud you and pat you and concede that you do indeed see the 'north' direction. But, then, for another creature, who sees from a southern angle, they will speak unto us, 'By Christ, we say, we see naught but a southerly direction!' Do we then disregard them?"

(Pause)

M: "So who speaks Truth then?"

W: *(Patiently)* "Both do, Man. For the creature who is from the northern angle, then what he does see, is a northern angle, and so for him, the 'north' is 'his' truth. And, as for the creature who locates himself in the southern location, then as for himself, his vision can only speak to him truthfully, that their vision is a southerly directed vision."

M: "So Truth has and have contradictory dualities that mutually oppose each other, and yet at the same moment, co-exist?"

W: "Correct, Man, for perhaps, you do now see some burning light, amidst this fiery blackness of this dead night of blackness?"

FINIS

∞

Passion

People
They kill
While dying
In an attitude
As they think
And yet
Never know.

❦

Passionate Evening

People!
Listening unto a painting's passion
Telling them of paths that may be taken
Will they then understand
The similarities of truth
While, in their own eyes, they may believe
In the everlasting colours
And of the distances within themselves
How, then, will the need for a passion emerge?
For your life can so become
As a liar's glance
Seeking nonsensical dances
Of meanings and postures.

For all that you may speak
In your life
And the truths that you struggle to love
Will you then accept the death of time
For you individually
Soon, to come;
In this candle before you that weeps
Seeing her own end
Come so suddenly
A light unto others
And a death unto herself.

❦

Pathetic Admission of a Failure

I loved
But I didn't succeed
That was
My truth
My fact
Liars are laughing
At the monkeys
That copy my every fabricated conceited twitch

What a bland show
I am never really anywhere
I am never where I am
And where I pretend to be
Really
I live now in this year 2002, June 1st
Within my self-induced stress
Of much
That is in my mind
And so,
That is why, I can't do much
Christ save me!
And I know that actually no one
Will really
Ever save me

And so, may my last
Breath
At the least
Be God's breath?

୬୯

Peace Shall Come

And peace serene
Speaking muffled whistles
'Neath hearts boiling
Whose tears are attempting the procedures of communications
Hands exasperating pointing violently at each other
At your talk which is an unmitigated catastrophe
As you try, yes
To succeed
And upon this scantily clad earth
People, Man, humans welcome
Welcome to this planet!
Hounded, persecuted forever
By dictums, sermons, paper, words
And peace
Somehow through twists and the mist
Shall come
Somehow we are to triumph though mired in blood rank
Within ourselves and our mind's consciousness
Circling and floating around sorrows
Speak up!
I scream, exposing my sanity to threats severe
Your eyes are already speaking these maniacal threats
If ever you knew
Speak of your intents, if you fear not exposure!
Divulge as ever and more, and allow yourself to be judged then!
Peace shall be;
Somehow and beyond what I was really meaning to be
Peace shall be;
Beyond what I have lived through and I say enough
May that be your peace
For all of you

☙

Philosopher of Modern Art

When questions pose meanings surreal
The answers question themselves
We, in our homes
Homes of nowhere
We questioned
We hoped melodies could mean
Meaningful truths
Somehow
Go home, now
Your home
There are no hopes, nor homes,
Your lives
Are dying, slowly
Go home!
Pay the drinker
To go home
Pay the last conversationalist
Pay yourself money
Express a smile now
She sits in front of you
Standing there
Doesn't she?
Boredom killed us now
Boredom killed art!
Unreal and surreal
Abstract and impressionist
Boredom killed art!
Your beloved and shallow art
Died, where
Humans died.

ଊଓ

Photograph That Caught It All

What a moment
Captured by the moment
Of a sudden shrill photograph
Heated hatreds
Frozen minutely
By chaotic minds & intentions
See that grin there
How blessed it sounds
And this angry tear shrieking silently there
From that abandoned boy
Who was trying to talk to you
Abstract memories
That I now and then colour my emotions with
As I lay down
And work
Alien friends
My wife is getting older
In her revulsion
Silently
Against myself and my putrid totality
I guess, yes
She needs
To axe me out
From her life
That is my seedy life
Low pay
And stinking breathless attempts to live
By smiling
Again
Serving stupidly and dying
All in one
That one photograph did capture it all
That one second of time
Its truths frozen forever

☙

Pidi
My beloved bird
My baby featherless bird
Now you are six years
Yawning eyes
Eating driblets of forsaken seeds
Christ I loved you
As I hugged you
In my frail arms
This
Explosively beautiful creation
Of God
Baby boy Izzet
I loved you so much
And yet
Any day
Your mother
May take you from me
Pidi
Pudu
I need you
My wonderful squirrel
You are the warmest furriest gerbil mouse
I have ever gotten to know
Baby Izzet
You talk
And I dream

৩৫

Portrait of a Life of a Selfish Theologian

Killers are killing lambs
Cunning Lovers are loving icon-seeking insecure humans;
And I see you
Praying to whom?
A godless mind?

Or is your 'god' a Godless God?
Or, is your God
A God for the Faithless?!
And you did not even notice -
When that soul-searching priest searing in his maniacal terrors
Suddenly sacrificed himself, shrieking
"I can no longer understand Life and its Insecurities!"
Yes, you scornfully snickered and said:
"I call it suicide! Weakling!"
Call him what you want
But I understood too much of his
Inner torments that were gashing and slicing
What Sanity was left within his atrophied body

In your blurred mind –
I – but wait, here
It didn't matter really
Since when do you ever
Talk to your own mind anyway?
So of what 'use' is there to
Communicate with you?

Remember that howling man who was
Always screaming so silently?
No one heard him
Least of all you, your self-satisfaction seeking Self
And your thoughtless ears
For, mutilations of men, women and children
Were too arduous a task for you to view,
Listen to and be compassionate
In an understanding and thoughtful manner;

And you know what?
You were never equipped for all these humanitarian situations
Where and when Humanity so glowingly suffered
So you continued with within callous, cold life
Where only what mattered
Was your Supremely Self Confident Arrogant Unfeeling Self.

ભ્ર

Pressures On an Unsure Mind

The struggling beauty
Sees herself
Painfully ugly
Insecure madness
Pressurising words
She writes
In some notebook
Struggling to understand
Trying to conquer her fears
The insane
Are suffering
I tell you
In my own mind
Vast oceans of strange smiles
I'm not sure of at all
Humans shady and in pressuring fogs
Are waving at us
Goodbye?
Is it?
I'm not sure really
But my fury remains
Dear Daddy
How much you suffered
I know now
In my wilderness
In the fiery Heavens you roam tonight
And eternally
While I slave for my appointed
Time here
On this struggling earth
When I read
I can see no sense

From the geniuses and academics
I read and
I feel nothing
How simple
And yet
You force us
To gobble your
Incomprehensible gibberish
By writers you tell us
Who are 'professionals'
But I laugh at all these medalled and honoured clowns
Do you know
What teaches me?
What does teach me
Is a tear
Of anyone
Ethical
Humane
Moral

෴

The Pretender

Sell
Your heart
As Coldness
Killed its Passion

A Passion
That was
Fake.

❧❧

Prostitute's Dream

A helping hand waves in distant appeals
While realities projected by liars
Transpire in hatred waxed and refined
The conversationalists' hollowness laughingly
Excused the wars individuals fight
While a prostitute yells
To godless martyrs
Who preached of Gods
As the dwarfs compared themselves
To the beauties of loneliness
The hungry painted ships of adventure
In their mysterious journeys, they asked:
"Where are we to go?"
The woman was betrayed
By the quick-tongued lover
Her eyes chased different circumstances
Forgetting that circumstances change
Therein lies the equation of human beings
Humans who care not
While the dying one
Strums
Her brittle
Guitar
Made of tender wood
Where the hollow tunes soon died
Her voice squeaked in No-Man's-Land
Her eyes, a sunset they revered
Her eyes that followed her lover's path.
Somewhere in a dark distance
Eyes rigid and fixed
Even though the winds sway you with pain
Your Protectors are dead, I declare!
Your Protector is no more
Understand that;
And understand your enemy
The one within you
Then shall you feel so much more
For alone you walk in this life
You breathe in.

⁊⁊

Pyramid Rock

And a fragment
Of a dying Rock, I took
To you I give a simple meaning
For I seek no expensive jewel
But the shred of human sorrow
Architecture of Cruelty that I can only despise
I offer you this gentle piece of pain
From thousands of years ago
Built by anonymous souls
Who loved as any Man could
Who dreamed of mansions for themselves
And yet were doomed to be entombed
Their withering minds
Building graves for unchosen masters;
Soaring stillness!
Surrounded by sorrow's bones
And scattered rocks, such as sweat never did see
And within a natural fragrance
The Extremes Man has gone to
Leads others to react in extremes
While an extreme of solitary beauty
Gazes upon us
And smiles quietly.

❦

Rain Hungers for the Thirsty Sand

The ambiguous greetings
Of an unsure, insensitive sun
That hurt
Her children who were bleeding.

Endless moments
Of a finger tearing torture
As you gouge this sensitive eye.

They laugh
From a chaos of truth
That reverberated in her half-hearted meanings
They spoke in their shadowy gestures
As a woman of ancient heroic proportions
Tried to die
In her disconsolate will
Lost by everyone
And saved by someone.

I write
As I can
In this land of cold freezing
Minds
We lived here
Just as our God wanted us to be
And then
These phrases were meant to
Awaken you.

Learn this much:
This rain
That hungers for a
Thirsty sand
Begging in a forsaken land
Of deserts
While you mindlessly call and echo
Out somewhere you know nothing of
In this Land of an End
Do you really think that is a solution?

೮೧

Raped Woman's Letter

When people their eyes speak
Of hatreds arithmetical
Driven by the mountains within you
Mountains of all burdens and sorrows
Understand all that you scream and say
Where the treasures in a truth are unravelling
Between the dialogue's empty path
Where an innocence shy weeps out its pain
Of childhoods all abandoned and forlorn
Surviving in your world
Painting your rules of self-deception
Drawing your smile's words
Words of defence
Where self-reflection
Is as a dagger perceived, distant yet fierce
For every moment where anger does seethe
Never can the evil, the bland undertaken be accepted
Obsessed by an idea or two purchased
From a land of ghosts and fakery
What then have you taught me in your lessons so vivid
Your lies and lives routine I see so clear
While pasts sometimes seem to close in
Killing our instincts to feel
For somewhere, my existence reckless has seemed
And the sweetness you all knew
Has died for a liberty so soon
As the vague storm screams: "Stranded!"
The wilderness within thereby does understand
Pulled and pushed by the hearts of a human satanic
Your speeches no longer fool the abstract
And serene.

಼಼

Red-Green Room

(Operating Theatre During Wartime)

In a room
Odours
Of a hundred
Recollections clear.

In a room
Darkened
By lust and sweat
It was
Soulful hatred
Serene
Operating true.

And there
With all the Manuals of Vice
Laid bare
Death's anatomy
Is dissected
By eyes bored
And poisoned blind.

And underneath all lay there
Crumpled sheets
Of soul's flesh
And humans ignored.

∞

Regrests of a Failure

I recall the sermons of my heart
That echoed in me
The fears that frightened me
So profoundly
I see
The trials that withered me
Artificialities, my friends
How did you understand it all?
All I saw were the doves that bled white blood
I read their raging lips that were so clenched
I heard their screams of sorrow
Yet, do imagine all the love that they gave
Their eyes, I did try to paint in canvases dry
Did you ever know my instances now?
Did you ever know as you forgot me so easily?
Yes I do recall the hours we loved and laughed
Our hearts, I remember, felt fibres sensitive
And maybe a failure I have been,
Yes, I do concede – I have failed true
Yet, still, through it all, I've loved
In my brief life, in my hours
These hours that have been so motionless and still
The icy weather that has so routinely
Frustrated my warmth
My vivacious passions
Have been torn shred by shred
And though my love filled ocean
Has myself dismissed
This life of mine has since become seriously non-sensical
No sense and no more any purpose,
So don't you fly now
Don't fly so far away from me!
For who knows where I myself shall be
In the years of tomorrow that will so surely be
Perhaps I shall for once be a man so true.

☙❧

Regrets

Goodbye
Tears of life
A farewell
Beckons
So I'll say
My words
Of today
While sincerely
Despising
My yesterdays
For my structure
And spelling
Were so wrong;
So often
Did I only
Listen
To words
I spoke.

❧

Rejoice

May joy cure all heartaches
May the chants, parades and tears
Burst your soul with fire alive
May the seeds of glory and martyrdom
Spring forth from the poundings of tyranny
May the countless weeping's and sorrows cease
For so at last
A direction-laden spirited wind harks
Oh! Awaken to the light –
Your chains melt now
And your faces glow with joyfulness
Never again to suffer...
Never again to agonize...
The moment sweeps the idle
And the mocking flee past their insignificance
Laugh and rejoice all ye people
Rejoice!

ଚଙ

Sad of the Earth

Tell me
Of the doomed
The sad
The sad of the earth
Tell me
Of the lonely ones
Scavenging holes
Tell me
The hurt ones
Where are they
I ask you all
The hungry, hidden souls painted years ago
Described years ago
Seen years ago
By you all
Where are they all
Tumbling around you
Struggling for the smile
Struggling for normalcy distant
Are they you
Are they within your hearts
I ask
Searching in this life
Life momentary
Pointless specks
Of flesh and stories
Yet, fiery stars we are

Beauties we all are
The lame
Beauties, I declare
The sick
Beauties, I declare
The sad
Beauties, I declare
I feel
You all
Must at some
Time see
Head in hands
Crying alone
Changes and confusion
Sanity's stillness
Fearful, I know
Unending themes
Swaying with no decency
The pretenders shall die
The oppressors shall die
I pray
Who will gently
Now tap those
With head in hands
Crying alone
Tell them of
The peace that shall come!

&⊙&

Sad Woman

While she drank
Her crusty eyes
Begging, aching to be needed
Her blue elbow
Sang tortured truths.

What we saw
Was too much
Before we dried our hearts
From a beginning
That just cried
To end now.

And she wept her needs out
Strangling words
From a dry, flaky, ragged skin;
So drink your empty drink
Till you can see
No longer
In this ending distant night
Of a coldness that cried
From your tired beliefs.

Staggering that early morning
Where someone just had to
Pick you up
From your oblivion
Sweet woman
Your crutches have withered
So long ago.

ॐ

Savage is Life

A question in me
Where senses dance
Tunes insane
Where imaginations
Caress skies heaving
Uncertain winds
Carrying fate
Of ours here
Sweetness, I seek
An image serene
A protector long dead
Where compassion
Is beingness
Where truth
Is passion
Within us
Tell the forgotten
Tell the despairing
Children of sorrow
Young and old
Savage is life
Savage it is!

ᏦᎧ

Saying Goodnight

Sweet night
Writing your fragile, tender words
For us
This aching night
Now ends
In her infant birth
Begging you all
To be near her
Just as the sudden farewell
Beckons you to be alive
From your sleep

Coming outside
Into a dusty breeze
We wait for our end
Adults of the night
Let us drink then
To this fall out
This end
That is in store for us
Just before we leave here
And we shall say our goodnights
To you
The living souls
And, they fetch their rotting manuscripts
To recall what they had to pronounce
And say
About themselves

Too soon
I say
You spoke.
Too soon, you laughed.
Too soon,
You concluded.

☙❧

Self Oppression Against Yourself

Those that greedily scorn you, they that persist in
Surrounding you and touching you;
Those that innately despise your Being, exist all around you
Screaming themselves to be your
'Friends', 'Lovers' and 'Family'
But, think, I speak to you -
For, you are alien in thought and appearance to them
You are their reminders of what they themselves cannot ever Be

You create these Reflections of Fright that breathes
In their intertwined ribs of Perversities;
Listen! For you are what?
You are the Symbol Painful of their Evil
For these Sickening Sinner, who
Whenever contemplating the Lucid Portrait
That you have painted
And that you have so effortlessly
Exposed to their sickened sadistic Brains
And, yes, they become terrified;
Terrified of what, you ask me?
They become severely frightened
Of themselves
And that is why they turn their cheeks
From their own Sadistic Selves
From the portrait of themselves
And they twist now on to another path
Far removed from their own realities
And they thereby
Continue
Their murderous work

Understand, then, the Dangerous Emptiness which is around you
Understand, then, the Culture of Stupidity that they have surfaced from
For theirs is the land of silliness too real to behold
Theirs is the Land of Self-Fear
This is the land of Stupidity
The Civilisation of Plasticity
The Culture of Brainless Beautiful Bodies

Nations totalitarian render masses fearful of authorities on all levels
Yes, how true, but wait!
Nations democratic render masses fearful of what is within each Soul
Their stolen identities, lost and gone
The Screams of Munch reverberate and pound and murmur and sigh daily
In their varied manifestations and voices
In their varied moods and appearances within your insides.

Fear of one's Self
The fear to discover human bonds, and not the norm
The fear to realize your need for Humanity, Warmth and Substance that
Cannot be attained
For, it does rarely reside in the homeland of the humans – the brain.

Yet, if loneliness and an island you become, you shall suffer accordingly
Social animals we are
Defective society turns your Personality, your Essence and your Being that is real
It turns and transforms you into the forests of Living Graves;
The same decomposing graves that are situated so deeply
Underground; and that lurk frightfully and mockingly
Within the sinister murkiness of your Disconnected Minds -
And then, you suffer necessarily, as you must, given your *Unreasonable Realities*
For, you are Alone and within Stillness, you exist
Existing in an open cage they call 'Life'
And I call Self Oppression

And your varied passions and necessary needs do not hear their echoes
Nor do you see the murmurs of meaningful eyes from anyone anymore.

A dilemma such as this, needs to be understood and replaced
With healing ideas, Sacred and Eternal in their Supreme Serenity;
I tell you, o souls, Spiritual and Meek;
Treat the waxy masks around you,
Who casually call themselves your 'Friends', your 'Lovers', your 'Family'
Treat them with your steel masks
Enjoy what you can enjoy
Try to nourish your bodily needs
There is no shame in that!

Even though they may be the driest fruits of your existence
For the recluse's life can lead to further pains and mental torture
Read, write, sing; these Essences and Activities shall help
With the slowed passages of time
Co-exist, inasmuch as you can
Inasmuch as your masks allow you to co-exist
For you know, there shall be a tomorrow for you
The years of weariness and withering wilderness, shall cease
Hope in a superior tomorrow is a jewel and an essence of Humanity
The Fabric of your Life is that Hope
Without it, you suffer being but bitter and dying in your living
In between miserable conflicting strands of emotions and behaviour.

෴

Sermon of a Dying Man

Tell the children needlessly orphaned
Tell them of their sorrows that have become listless
Have a mercy on yourselves, your insights that drum out no instincts
The weightless brains that still speak in eyes mournful
All do believe in their pointless ghosts as they twist their hopes and feelings
To accommodate what they do not even understand
Not even a drunken clown can praise this existence, for none will even understand anyway
And that was the closest moment humans edged near the truth's meanings
While dancers with skulls of infantilism unbearable expected their dues in their manufactured lives
Manufactured by experiences plastic
Go check and see the prisoners and their unending days for the crimes they have not done
Look at the self proclaimed darling of the evening who sincerely believes in herself for this hour
anyway
As the men gaze in profound admiration I called lust
And what can I myself say to you, dear lady, when I only see your
Unmet needs, your undernourished mind?
Yes, I did see in my mind once while you stood there with your carnival people
Your carnival culture of emptiness that so burdens the yearning, needing soul
I spit at you 'humans' defined all along by depraved cultures
I saw believing cretins stabbing furiously at all that they deemed unworthy of their lofty visions
Hurling insults that they themselves had no problem loving
The stars, I see, are fading, their loving messages have sincerely grown weary of your humanity
downstairs
I see the skies blackening, revealing the few that still bother to glitter
Still willing to address 'humans' upon this oppressive planet
Show us, you stars out there, show us!
The blind witnesses who craftily fabricated our cultures of lies and sins
Reveal unto us, o stars out there, so far, far away
Reveal to us the witnesses who cooked the blandest lives, minds and personalities of people
everywhere
Such, I tell you, are the severe manifestations of the alienating lives in their mindless contexts
Whose minds I peep at staring feverishly at empty holes and trying to discover emptiness itself!
These wrecks are still hoping that somehow their lives will be joyous voyages
Tell them the truths, ye 'humans' out there, if you can be faithful for a while
Tell them of the wildernesses that constitute your civilizations
Tell them of the raging insecurities, the despairing frustrations of Mankind as they oversee their
brittle hopes

Tell them of the monumental mountains of tears that have stained your entire histories
Tell them the words, the scripts of the abandoned ones who screamed repeatedly: "Save our minds
from these humans of yours!"
The times have crippled the masts of your ships
And the storm's intents, you do not know
Nor could you ever guess
So, waiting, you labour under these psychotic storms that will surely sway you too some hour soon
The criminals may have already raised their banners of victory as you struggled to fight for serenity
But it was not to be
Herein I tell you is what existence is all about: the triumph of injustice over the just
Though you all still need that loving, warm touch
The meaningful care
You all need allies you call 'friends' and 'lovers'
Do not, then, be disappointed with failure
Just look above and you shall see the birds mocking you heartily
Look for once in your bleak lives, look at the faces of humans, and see their true colours
When they speak of their certain words, tell me what they spoke in truth
When they hold you in affection, tell me what temperature did you feel in them
And only then, turn to yourselves
And realize the truths of this world and its lives you live within!

ᏭᏮ

Sermon of a Troubled Woman

I tell you
Of the sorrows
Within us,
Yes
I am trying
In us all
For a just passion
To reign

I know a sadness is covering
Vast expanses inside and beyond us
Yes, I still try to speak to you
After all, my needs are your needs!
For are we not one soul
Within us all?

Could you and I paint a hope believable?
Can you and I here and now hear the distant melody of right?
Tell me, what an otherwise can there be?
We are all alone, my friends
Didn't you know?
My friendless friends, didn't you guess?

Bless the humble
Bless the sorrowful
Bless the sad of the earth
Bless those who are ignored and dying within us all
Here, now and for the inexplicable future, I say
Love the sad
Love the forgotten
Love the shy ones
Love the isolated ones
Love those unable to speak out aloud
Love those unable to protest and scream
Remember the unheard ones
Remember the dead
Remember the refugees
Remember those with anxieties and severe panic
Remember those with thorns in their feet

In all countries and in all lands where life precariously lives on for now
I beg forgiveness for the ones laden with power
I weep for the stabbed ones
I weep for the cheated ones
I weep for the humiliated ones
I weep for the hurt ones
Understand them and understand their sick oppressors

See the self-assured, joyous angels in the ceilings of your minds
In their paths of wisdom and pleasure, both loving and secure
And, you, now, see the stark mirror staring at you
Staring at you all these times, didn't you know?
I knew that was my message and my letter to you

To those who saw far too much
To those who have repeatedly been punched, kicked and slapped
I tried to explain to you
In my limited life
Limited by my own mental manacles
What? Goodness!
Are you seriously surprised?
Ah! But you ought to have known, my friends!
Somehow I deemed all others would understand
Somehow to be more understanding
I guess I myself misunderstood it all.

ᐤᐤ

Severe Despair of the Innocent Girl

I love you
Child
Of mine
I can only love
This much
Before my finality appears

I am losing
My soul's Mind
Here within, hidden from you all;
I am trying
To speak sense
While frantically fearing my simmering Self

So, listen then, listen
You, who feel it only too worthy
To refuse my words -
Where then
Can I ever go
Now that
I am nowhere
In my earthly life?

ॐ

Simple Declaration

When
I recede
To a destined end
Do not weep
Though it is a natural reaction
But remember
What I went through
You did, too
For life is dismal
And death is freedom
Friendships do not exist
Love does not exist
Marriage does not exist
Families do not exist
I know
Those are your beloved icons
I know
That you feverishly believe in
But I tell you
These concepts
Are political
Based on self-interests

৪৫

Sin of Begging

Please believe
That maybe
An angel of little significance
May come
To steal
This, my begging hand
Away
And soon
I'll be far, far
Away
In a peaceful
Land of happiness
I say
I think
In my mind
I have tried
To realize
My ambitions of love
While truths
Annoy me
Remind me
At all times
Of my mistaken paths
Still, I tried to swim
Blindly through
Somewhere, somehow
An angel with blind eyes
Is looking for me, perhaps
And, maybe, if I try
And if you try
Maybe we can meet
Anywhere far from here my life!
O angel somewhere!
Please;
Save my mind
From this corrupting skin.

☙❧

Sins Beneath Vincent's Starry Night

A Drunken King wept over self-created sins
In his unglamorous life
The corrupt Wedding saddened
The thousand year-old Trees
Burdened by the Cynical Winds
Where Shy Priests
Doubted
Their edict's worth
That they copied all their lives

The Mature Virgin dreamed of lush meadows
Painted and imagined by the Quiet Madman
Where the Illiterates
Cursed aloud
At their colourful tears
That no one could decipher nor understand
As Panting Stars
Spoke
Of their daring homecoming

Scattered Women were venturing out at last
Unashamed to defy fear and threats from within
And Lovers awoke to their hypocrisy
Amidst Family Smiles
And the routinization of boredom
As Beggars of Humanity pleaded
Quietly
For Mercy
And no more abstractions

Distant Stars were swayed by Heavens
Troubled, once more, by us.
The Shining Hope shivers its warning for all hearts
To feel for themselves
In punishments they mentioned too often
Only for the Poor, the Lame and the Meek

In Unruly Nights soured in veiled darkness's
By the Anger of the Dying
Such crimes of the past were recalled
By the minds of the Cold Ones still ruling over you;
You Inheritors of a unique and particular grief
Where Colourless Eyes stare
At your simple
And Unanswered Passions
Yet, the pained and Insecure Citizen begs the
Starry Night to inspire
Fearing your Frightened 'Self'
You search all the other Selves
As a Conversation is repeated again
In your evenings of darkening anxiety
The gates of weariness burn
As I fear to tell and speak and relate any longer.

ༀ

Smile of Reason

Witness the word
Of God that smiles
On reason's passion,
Believing in a time
That you can predict
For yourself
Can never to be,
If only your eyes
Can glimpse!

For all the manners you display
Can you discern the
Traps
Being set upon this stage
Of a theatrical horror, called
Your 'life'?
In your wisdom,
You can beseech
For all the birds to love you
In their joyous paths
Of pleasure
And poise;

You see, right across your skies at night
You laugh now,
At the joker's nightmare
Becoming, a reality
To you,
And you can only accept your
World
If they are to be in tune
Within you,
Listen, then, to the smile of reason;
I tell you,
For all these gems that you speak of
Them, that need;
I now tell you
Tell them, to be silenced –
For they have not, for now,
Understood the unseen world.

ॐ

So Near, Yet So Far

Upon whom is the Passage
Safe?
The Passage of Life
Trapped
You stand insecure
Unsure, fearful
Within the nearness
Of truth
You are
And yet,
Stranded, startled
Frozen
You cry?

࿇

Sons of Adam

When I am
In this hour that stares at me
And whenever I speak
I turn and pluck out my brain
Into shrivelled fragments of frightened pain
This end
Is my beginning
From this dim, icy room
I eat my life
Within and throughout
I just invite you all
But I'm getting nowhere
In my own attempts
To live with you all
Sons of Adam

&c.

Speak Out, if You Dare

All heroes
Are you
Standing
to crumble
Weeping
To die
It is your
Life
And you knew.
Say your voice
I say
Because I may not
The hunger is beginning
And I am listening
Between my selves
Inside, elusive
And going far beyond.
People of an earth
Hearing announcements
You cannot feel
Listening to deafness
You cannot feel
Yes I can believe
In holes of hatred
Believe in them that are angry
Hating
If you can understand.

৪৫

Speaking Statue

Into this world, we wait
And our eagerness sways us
So much
Within repressed breasts
This world and life
Are threatened even more

The beauty of mine
No longer stands
Sorrowful and distant she beckons
Eyeless and chained

❧

Speech Of A Woman

I have no real, genuine memories
I can claim to have shared
With any of you;
Yes, don't be surprised –
What a vile world
I lived through
With you all
Who remember me!

Those sham expressive faces
Your zealous vacant smiles,
Delightfully inert conversations
Phony, convincing under nourishing passions
I played again and again, repeatedly
For everyone's pleasures

My senses chose to create
Forged humans within my minds
Who then played with you all
So unproblematic was it for me
You now see it was for my good self
To manipulate and stage-manage
You men and women I interacted with

And, yes, you are correct
Linguistics, cultures and backgrounds
Were no barriers for my minds
The plastic and the bone-like
Wooden ones;
And if I needed
To break, and smash
Your entirety
You Soulless Beings
Descendants of Adam and Eve
If I need to,
Yes, if necessary
I chose to
Change,
I chose to annihilate
Your criminal emotions
Your sinful motives to exist
Word by word
Bone by bone

Crumb by crumb of your
Entire physicality
Until I felt
My needs
Were satiated.

Am I
A fake?
Am I
'Inhuman'?
What Twaddle!
Listen to me you all
Faceless individuals of no
Convincing individuality:
My real faces, my minds, I do not share
My own discrete, unknown craving vices
My own veiled unsatisfied hunger and
Its longing requirements
Remain hidden
From you humans –
And good that they all be and remain so!
So how can I still
Be so much entertainment for you all?

Yes, I am a lady of eyes
That love
To stare
Your inquiries away
And yes, I adore
Staring at
Your spirits till
They decay
Away

You feel I am Arrogant?
And never more humble a whisper
Have I ever met
Like myself.

Why?
Because Life is a servants' game of chances
Wherein we flit in and out
That's what I do so casually well

You want to know how I operated?
I fixate all my obsessions vividly and clearly

Against any opponent I feel
Needs to be extinguished
Those words inside me remain
Trapped
Because I choose for them to be trapped

And I'll wait for you too
To make sure, I will see you
And sure you
Will crumble back to where you all began: dust

O my dear
I am alive!
And you?
Are
You Alive?
You think so?
You believe so?
Listen severely here to me;
Your sanity is vague, I remind you
And your ways and wages so mean
Your life is so distant
From your reality
While your worries so near to you remain tied
And all that you may give to Humanity
And all that you may share with Decency
None will care!
All shall
Remain alone, untouched,
Occasionally broken down in tears
Forever in that moronic
Game
You classify
As 'Living'
And I call 'Dying'.

ॐ

Stalin's Private Thoughts

Do not question the silly executioner
Executing the carcasses, the slabs of your relatives
The relatives of your lovers
The lovers of your parents
The parents of your children
The children of orphans
He only takes orders
He is the expendable worm
And I am the eternal Eagle

Excuse the rot that has surfaced
But that was never my fault!
Wasn't rot your Czarist aristocratic 'culture' that needed severe cleansing?
Because your civilisation proudly defecates excessively
In idiotic mouths loving and therefrom producing frothy sleaze
And so I, the cobbler's son, came to deliver you from this putrid stench

And the disorientated, destructive ones, you still claim, are your 'friends'
While I cannot ever accept the lives of such 'friends',
And capitalist whores are your lovers?
Do you expect me to accept that?
No, I must exterminate that class of scum humans
Look, I sincerely tell you
When not much is of any depth to me in your perverted society
What praise can I then speak of?
You always keep on asking me, 'Where's your mercy, Koba?'
You all must be seriously insane
What mercy can you ever expect from me?
In politics and life, Mercy only retards Progress
And Mercy for who, you fools?
Mercy for the frenzied psychopathic wreckers
Who are fanatically determined to destroy us all?
Now you may understand why
So much mass obliteration
Of men, women and children was, and is so necessary

Picture the story of science, history and politics all intertwined
To produce elegant truths on the paths for progress for all,
Picture the truth of the mechanics of History
The glory of Science and History marching heroically forward towards
The progressive communal society we all dream and need as proper humans
Wherein, yes supremely painful injections will be required
But wait – and you shall see the glorious results
No surgeon fears blood
No butcher fears slabs of squabbling unwanted meat
To forge a nation, I need blood from you humans
And for that end, I'll seek every end and means

I am, of course, expecting, that you are attempting
To speak the truth in your daily lives
Well, what is wrong with us
I ask you all;
Every time I speak
All we hear are the cynical sarcasms of you all?
People like that must be done with!
All of them!
You accuse me, "Koba! You're a Mass Murderer!"
And why am I so, I ask you?
"Because you butchered tens of millions of innocent people!"
Yes, I did so do
But that was my bill for this gigantic act of surgery
Because, comrades, your intellectual sarcasm and mockery will get us nowhere;
You see we do not have much time, do we?
Mother Russia must move fast
To mercilessly annihilate the wreckers
Time is against us
Or they will wreck us to extinction!

Beliefs in politically romantic ideas have vanished
You must have known
Across mine and your own experiences, memories over the years
In Siberian prisons and the gallows
Where we Bolsheviks suffered hurt, insecurity and loneliness
Where we met ignorant humans claiming to be literate
Buffoons!
How can you even try to properly speak to them?
How can you speak to them, when they threaten your every minute of your life?
That is absurd!
I am trying to believe in you all
People, society, masses, proletarians, peasants before me
But betrayal is our local currency here –
So what other act do you expect from me to entertain?
You thought I never worked this out?
I have never been fooled, but by God, yes have I fooled you again and again
I have fooled you
Right to your necessary deaths
And that is why, there is nothing more to do
Except to fight blood with the bitterest, foulest blood, I say
Until we achieve our supremely egalitarian Motherland.

෪෬

Strange Thoughts

I think I gave much of the bits I had
I made mistakes thinking my heart was
Concerned for her
But she was different from me
We possessed nothing within us
She was south
I was north
Nothing joined to and with
Nothing being our basis
For togetherness and love
She said greetings
I heard goodbye

Hatreds grew
And purities faded
Do you see
Scared scarred faces
Hiding
Behind
Veils of indecency?
Did they mean anything to you?

How immeasurable
Do sins hurt
Children?
Yes I know
I cannot count
What Sorrow means
To a
Child;

Quantify hurt everywhere
And you yield weighty oceans of savaged tears
And yes you can soon calculate the
Measures of quantifiable Anger

And soon
Just maybe
Revenge
Shall come

A man thinks endlessly of trying to find truth
I keep telling his darkening ear:
"You're being just too late!
"Truth
"Passed away indifferent in its countenance
"Just and only
"A FEW
"Centuries ago from your sad
"Hamlet".

ೲ

Streets of a Civilized City

On a street
Of Manic Prostitutes
Living through their really specialised Carnivals
Each offering
Specialities, fetishes
That only they themselves can perform

Christ!
I am being bewildered by all this talent and artistry
That is amazing even the paedophile priests
Who consistently smile
And persist in their words and Deeds

See the bleeding and mournful Christ
Gazing grievously at these Dirges
By a decapitated Humanity
Whose only real needs
Lie discarded

The liars are just beginning to lie
As the drugged psychiatrists, businessmen and politicians
Sharpen their latest weapons
Of torture;
Can I ever understand these feelings
I guess not
I can't –
But I do know
They're all out there
Celebrating this Unholy Night
Of murder, whoredom and sin!
Where endless processions of satanic laughter
Swirls
In and around people's smiles!

Christ!
Is it too tempting for some?
I guess
We're suffering so much
And there's just nowhere to be found
The right medicine
To cure our madness.

ॐ

Streets of Boston During University Days

In all the city
The skies darkened, cloudy and drizzle
Echoes of disturbed voices I see
Children's fears I feel
In pavements of another freezing morning
Walking to dreary work
Working to die
And the money is not there
And rent is high
And drugs are an excitement
In this city of yours
In this ugly room you live within
Cars numbingly passing by
You watch endlessly for no reason
Routine passions come and go
Promises written, torn and scratched to oblivion
Br friends, relatives and lovers who never knew
Who they were supposed to be,
Serious memories easily forgotten
In this icy city of Boston
The woman is no longer
With your sad face
In this, the wilderness of concrete slabs proudly called architecture
Anonymous workers walking on and everywhere
Yearning for love and passion
While the chefs busily cook on
For the glamorous wealthy and the governing officials
And fat is thereby increasing
While hunger is deepening
In all of our hearts
In the streets of icy, damp Boston.

ॐ

Stubborn Recluse

You stand
In this
One-sided truth
Quietly sad
In an eye
Of angry hurt
You may see
This moment
That passes
You by
Years ago
A thriving child
You were
And for now
Fading wrinkles
As you pass out
In this earth
You mistook for
A hell
Listen, Man;
My truth
Begs yours
To release this bird

Caged in your mind;
And let one half,
Meet the other
Half :

For you can't live otherwise,
And you can't try otherwise,
You stand alone
Determined!
In your truth
While you fade
From us all
You observe expressions of laughter
That we manufacture for the pleasant night
So you feel some light
But you remain alone
Returning to a home
No one knew of
And now
Now even the light
Is waving goodbye to you!
Doesn't it seem
They all are waving
Goodbye to you?
Doesn't it all seem
They all are waving farewell to you?
Listen, soul;
It is you
Waving that farewell
To your self
While we stand and watch.

❦

Stupid of This Earth

Welcome yourself to this world
Your land
This planet
I just wonder
Of all your plans ahead
Of the starlit Heavens that are simply beyond the grasp of your imagination
The sincere starlight which society severed severely
Did you hear it being said
You are stupid, face it?
Stupid beyond limits or beliefs
Face it
Your type governs this world
Runs governments and hospitals
Runs universities and television and newspapers
Runs brains and minds and all!
Stupid of the earth, why are you so united?

&

Stupidities of Life – As We Practice It

Everywhere people scurry and try to
Converse
Through jumbled verses and strange verbs
Getting vividly excited by
The essence of pointlessness
And seething energies are being lavishly spent
On idle, bland, tasteless matters
That do not
Mean much really
While young girls
Frantically parade
Their disjointed make-uped sexuality
In their solemn ambitious attempts to be
Serious women
And the hard thinkers confound themselves repeatedly
With their
Blaring insecurities
And exasperations at not arriving
At any logical answers;
I see endless psychiatrists
Venomously cold
In their trashy assessments
Lecturing the most idiotic
Counselling advice
While seriously suffering hands
Desperately thirsty for any
Helping love –
I tell you
That sick prostitute I spoke to last night
Spoke of society's hypocrisies
She did
Mean much to me.

ভৈ

Such is Earth

Lack of trust
Paranoid stares
Unfeeling whispers
A chance missed again
With no opportunities left
A strange gathering
Hysterical calm
Tears of admirers
Whilst clowns fade away
Such is destiny.

Castles of wounds
Slabs of youth
Monuments in shame
Burdened by chaos.
Rhythm faltering –
Trembling structures
Raising their voices
Struggling for their coordination.

This then is our words
So strange to you it seems
But such is earth
Such is fate
This then are our painted words
For you to review
Man's grace and humanity
Such is earth!
Such is fate!

༺༻

Sudden Slow Evening

So quiet
Sudden slow
Evening
I am
Alone
Bruised adult
I stand
To lose
And I'll be so fallen
As you
Look at
Me
Just as I
Die
In front of your
Smiles.

Sweetness
My life
Is so
Betrayed
Just as I
Wash my
Own hurt
That tries
To escape from
Its own
Rage

Sudden eye!
That looks
To try
To stare
At a Deceiving Truth;
Can you then
Ever understand
Me?

ॐ

Sudden Suicide

Eyeless mask
Ugly night
Going somewhere
She thought
Sudden knife
You pose
At your nerve
Killing madness
And ending
All discourse

෨෬

Suicidal Jack

In my bleakest hour
I never guessed
When it would all end
I never knew
If it would ever end
I just never knew
Because there were no signs
Telling me
Of a hope
I've been through
In blackness' blackest excrement
And yet
No one
Has ever
As yet
Shown
Hope to me
So I endured
The sickest endurance
And I suffered further
So now, when will my darkness
Cease
I just don't know
I really
Don't know
And it hurts like hell
It burns me too much
Melting my Sanity
Into hopelessness
Making it all pointless
To go on
Existing anymore.

ᕲᕲ

Suicidal Lover

And in truth
A pleasure
Whispers to me
'Wasn't your life sorrowful hurt?'
She breathed her question to me
What can I ever reply?
'Sweetness, my Death!' I speak
'My tomb shall be filled'
Tonight perhaps
But my fear clings still
You ask me, 'Did you hate?'
Yes, I did!
I did hate!
That was my fearsome Sin, yes
But where will I be, O Death were I to follow you
Through this still night?
My fear is screaming at my thoughts
For you!
For, yes,
I need to be free
And yes,
I say to you, let it be
Whatever your concerns may be for me -
Speak to me of your hidden dreams for me
And I will try hard to believe in you, O smiling sweet Death
Just before I am to die
Come to me!
Why is it I cannot see you?
When you desire to release me from bondage on earth
From my misery
Why is it I can't see your face, O Death?

೮೧

Suicide is Painless (1)

You hear so much of love
They tell me they see it every day
But I do not
As I talk or mumble
About statistics, fear, loneliness, failure
I have
A small rancid micro chamber in my heart
That houses evil strangers
That pulses bloodily with disturbed emotions
That cries at times with panicking
Vigorous mental fear and
Physical pain

I feel hypothermic
Frozen
Numbed
And my love for you
Is a slow denial
Of my life
Because of who you are;
Sweet heaven
I continue to exist
In an sticky hour
In a sorrowing moment
In a blurred town
But what does that
All mean to you
Nothing.

I speak, though I am empty
I am frail, though I pretend virility
Sweet one
Crumbling I am!
Yet I keep going on and on
As I make myself stare
At you
All in all
I guess
I ask myself
I can only go on living
If there is hope
This will someday end
For, otherwise
Where's the worthiness
In this type of
Life?

છ

Suicide is Painless (2)

Come now
Into my eyes
As I decide
To depart
From my only
Remaining
Sorrow moments.
Beautiful hate
Hating life
Can you
Then
Ever
Feel me
Here
Just as I
Decrease
Myself?
And I can only
So much
Now give
In my
Ending appearance
I could only
Hate.

Anatomist Poet ᘒ 297

Suicide of a Woman

Killing
Your only
Haunted eye
And those that witnessed
How frail
You are
Yawn
O! How vile Man is!

And if hell
Were to breathe
So within
Your failing language
Yet again
Then, understand
That your ending truths
Within your faltering self
Is nearing.

How much you did suffer
Can ever a Man guess?
Or feel?
Just as you succumb now
I tell you,
No one can
Or will
Feel for you
Sweet.

உ௸

Suicide of a Young Woman

Please help me
I can only give
So much of my heart
That stood there selfless
Burning for you

It's all an ending for myself
I'm losing
My life
My mind and soul
I'm going out
Now

You've seen
My pages
That may have been read
Well,
What does it matter now?
Christ!
Your blood
Just satisfied no one!

Everywhere
I'm being hounded by fear
That threatens me, Sir, God;
Please now
Forgive me
I think
Sir,
I've been hurt
Now quite
Beyond belief

I think,
I've just had enough
Of all of this
You call
'Life'
Here
And now

౪

Suicide of an Intelligent Girl

Abrupt instant
Surfaces here
As I write my
Own bloodied script
That speaks
Of my animated
Lives

I see faces whose needs
Are criticizing their
Self-less children

Just as I reduce
Myself
To a pointless
Second
Of such
Menace

Can you ever imagine me
Just as I
Drive my own
Continuation
To a quiet
Edge?

&

Suicide

Sweetness
I live
From my breath
That severely recedes
In her submissive finality
That weeps critically
In her self-tearing soul
Mangling hatreds
Just getting no
Where
In my truth
My self
That angers me
I guess
And I guess
So much
I stand alone
To die
Empty and shattered
Empty pieces shattering
Within myself
Fragmenting emptiness
As I sit for
My cherished self
Unknown idiot
Hurting my mind's gazes
And dying by my side
Forgotten
In between these pages
Pointless poetry
I die to bring myself
This supreme
End
Turning inward
Makes me believe in
This fateful death
Lonely escapes
From a truthful sky
That calmly tried to tell me
"Come hither, soul!"

ରୈ

Suicide Statistics

A priest wept!
Hidden in his black garments
A sword, he thrust inwards
And blood exited sadly
But intentionally
Priests of suicide
Their sorrows outmatching their sermon's logic.

A clown etched an epitaph
Inscribed the clown:
'Died the priest for feeling futility'
And the clown laughed for the first time.

Smiling politician!
Seeking words to self-aggrandise himself
Collecting money
Shaking hands
Left and right
And preached on suicide's statistics
In his weekly lecture to a troubled nation
Yells rang! "Tell us your mind, politician!"
Astounded at this reaction
He turned away and laughed
The die-hards firmly applauded
While the echoes of ignorance
Were once again heard
'Cross a disturbed and slumbering nation.

৪৫

Suicide's Thought

Who thinks of his worth
And what does it all add up to
If anything
And should it add up to nothing
Then shouldn't we extinguish it all
And so get away and far from this
Lie you all call
Life?
Isn't it a sinister mocking
Blistering insult
Perpetrated against our tongues
And broken throats
Woman
I spoke to you
So many times
Didn't I?

&

Suspicious Soul

The liars
With their painted minds
I see their sickly, evil winks
How, then, can you ever fault me
As I live
In this damnation
You call earth?
Existing corpses all around me
Withering and decomposing imperceptibly
Didn't you guess
What they need from you all?
Look at all those oceanic ugly sea spirits
Screaming at me daily
Battering me daily
And you passionate followers of abstractions immaterial laughed even more
Laughing, waiting for my death
I swear,
I saw;
I realized.
Don't be too busy here
Humans tell me
Don't be too attached
To those who suffer
Within their lives of failure
Were they describing me?
I could not hear clearly
For there was far too much
Shrieks and laughter hysterical.
Beings are being deformed by raging air and drowning, drunk winds
Everyone
Has to cry
In order to live!
Cry to live now
As everyone abandons everyone
Disguise your foolish smiles
I say
I speak now
What you feel, what you experience you humans
Are irrelevant
You are all irrelevant!

☙❧

Sweating Statues

Statues swerving in rooms well disguised
In portraits the naked deride
Where moments past died fast
"Please save your laughs", you heard entranced
"Please save your laughs", you heard entranced.

Gathering fortunes, the useless said
In distances un-heard the days ached
And saving their ways, they soon learned
Their paths; ways and routes:
O so moments past!
And o so moments past!

☙❧

Sweet Remote Friendless Friend

And from a sad
Beginning
The beggar
Ate his
Only word
Of sudden hope
That so surrendered
In that meagre life
Of Despair
Sweet remote friendless friend
I wrote to you
To guess, and ever more
At you
Intentions and whims
We so did, then
Exist
In this expensive desert
Of life
Your last
Life.

❧

Talking to a Suicidal Woman

Too good?
My truths and needs are being
Remanufactured
By recluses
Who were smiling
In front of fake mirrors
Produced by self deceiving professional liars

'What can I do with you?' I asked you so many times
But you always gave me such
Twisted answers
With the logic of Satan
You thought
My rationality was being coy
But it wasn't, my dearest
It was just my absurdities

And yet
We had all to live
Within these
Claustrophobic days
And pointless heated discussions
With their excessive baggage of tears
And rages
That duly achieved a naught

I saw nothing but more of my depressions
That seemed like snarling waves too me
Seriously trying to murder myself
Coming and going
But always returning
And maybe succeeding soon with myself?

❦

The Advice of a Sage Woman

A woman came
From Nowhere to speak
To Men.

"I speak of colours aplenty
Have I tempted thee?
Your scattered ears laugh at me
Your directionless wind whistles in unruly anger
So listen to me, my children
Think not I have come to tempt you
Listen hard to me

For your sufferings
I tell you
Shall not cease
I am so sorry
For I have no better words for your lives
You have perhaps seen the unread pages of History
These stories are being played out today
In your very own lives
On your soil that you tread on
Repetition is the essence of History
And all will truly be forgotten
Your blindness will condemn your sad Destiny fast!"

Then, the Woman wept and begged to be heard
While the learned Men walked on
In paths they knew nothing of.

ॐ

The Anonymous Letter Signed 'Sarah'

The death of a stranger
Who once cried in the streets of cold
And yet wrote words of hope

As I ached for a spiritual sleep
Wherein such cruel mornings awakened us all
The meanings of my passions were lost
Their motives became unknown to me

While the crowds gathered their lives
In processions dictated
At a predetermined hour
They gathered to sing futile prayers
As the storms of boredom swept the anxious ones
Their passions
Were masked forever more
                              - Sarah

☙❧

The Atheist Priest

A word, my friend, I spoke
Where angels of my father's memories called
Where mother's weepings sang tunes in my mind
Never could I ignore these essays that affect humans
Where throats hurt once more
And dryness cuts sincerely
How could a clown cry, I gasped?
Here, and forever more, I thought
Wilderness shall be my highway
Endless in repercussions and threats vague
Where sentences are spoken by the distracted and unreal
I complain unto no one
Yet, still, I complain into a god I believed in once
A god, I thought, could change and alter the laws of physics
Alas, for now, dryness hurts my memory as I attempt
To recall 'exact' images of my friends
Where hollow skies
And where thorny verses preached
Where smiling lies convinced us true
I look at sands cold and snowy
I stand by now
Here
I stand by watching.

&&

The Barren Skulls

April 26, 1989 – Boston
A chance unexpected
The door closed
Unseen opportunity
Darling woman
Life's statues that I see
I'm hearing fading music
Look on
Look ahead
The winds will twist soon
Their paths never understood
No day
No day is the same
They tell me
And tomorrow will present you with new events
I can't believe too much
Preach to the donkeys
Ugly beasts of burden
Feel the sorrow for the suffocated and ignored
And who looks at who?
In this planet here
Planet revolving
And my life is stationary, I swear
So the chances come in like coincidences
Whilst the dancer explained her motions
To senile judges
Sensuality embraced the barren skulls that preside over us
How fair, my God
Time and again
The night wanderer prayer for water
The deserts howled in windy laughter
And another dancer reeked with sorrow
Dance of the sand storms
Poor souls, poor families
What you're needing
It's all so fading
What you desire
It's all been stolen years ago
Your gods, your idols
Seek revenge against them
Only then will your journeys and sensualities
Have meaning.

☙❧

The Conversation

And when I saw him
I said, "Speak to me with the Eyes of Man!"
What elderly whispers therein slept
Eyes of seventy or eighty years ago
What dust and tears you have carried with you
What landscapes you have journeyed into;
While I am an image for you
Of this ending Western Century
Hold my hand
And I will be just like you
But you walked
So fast
By me
And never more
Will we ever meet.

There is nothing to speak
When
In this silence
Man was taught
This word
That defined Emotional Essence
Still you and Man sit
Motionless
In this land they called Vague, Uncertain Life.

Speak what your eyes saw, I say
Speak to these yawning listeners here
These listeners
Who have seen the animated fractured truths
So you will stand to be corrected
Or not;
Remember:
This life that ebbs from you
Has warned and thanked you
So now, you and your tears
Break your silence
And speak now.

Legless night
Armless truth
Beggars' eyes
Pleading to need

This silly crumb of your
Love
Will you pass it on
As I sit here dreary night
Lonely moon
You're all out there
Alone
Educating this black night
Here, there's coldness
Stillness
Please believe me, now
As I unravel and wither
Here, in my own days
Days of many days
Coldened hearts, trying to get warm
We really tried to love
Betrayed by Man and his smiles
We tried too hard to get near
To wasted glamour
And an overused sexuality
Idiot minds of ours
Listening to failure's books
We played so soft
In a war that was
Amputating our
Sensitive eyes
I can now only turn inwards
As I fade out
From this world and its breathing life
We'll all forget each other
So, goodnight tonight.

൭൭

The Dead Relationship

Down a corner
An alley you see
Hunger spits at me
And the laughing woman
Dresses in cards of gold
People assume what is of value
Here, on this planet, this fancy club, this room
They all understand vaguely the needs
And all act thereby
But where does the inter-relationship act
Itself out?
Not in your life
You will forget most of it
And you will laugh, as you must
Dear Unknown Friend
This is what I see
In this night of ours shared
The corners of the world
Never existed
Save in our needs for convenience
And so
Walk down that corner
That same alley
Where a hunger may spit at you
Too.

ഔ

The Deer, the Dove, the Wolf and the Haunted Children

I hear whispers breathing memories
I hear and see the historic trails
That was the work of Man
Bloodshed and more blood
How odd I thought
A deer finally committed suicide
Her beauty was never understood
Her wisdom was never gathered
Yet, the wolf wisely argued
"What passion did you seek?"
The deer never listened to the wolf's advice
For the deer was far too frightened
Of the intentions of the wolf
And so never did
Have the chance of understanding
The wisdom of the wolf's words

Twenty eight doves of peace
Drowned in a stormy sea of tumultuous emotions
In an ocean of heaving misunderstandings
And in the existence of profound confusions
The sad lives of the doves and the deer
Intertwined
While human chaos continued unabated
Where, exactly, where you doves going?
What passions did you want us to feel?
Did you want to speak to us about Love?

Twenty years ahead
I witnessed wars and hatreds
In civilized lands, I swear to you
Where murder was defined as abstract
And where mass murder
Was produced with an abrupt, curt nod
A nod of no essence
And yes, I saw the haunted eyes of children
Spitting at me the vilest accusations
Demanding to know: Where my Humanity existed?
These were, after all, the Children of Humanity!
I only felt sorry for them all
What 'Humanity' were they talking about?

ରଙ

The Empty Human

All your conversations, they can go on
For all the time, that one can listen
Hearing words of the Master and the Slave
How could you continue this lie of living loneliness?
In your empty mansions
The truths are all waiting for you
And you continue
In your diary of professional nothingness
But, you hurt!
The only one who can tell you
And judge you so truly within
The emptiness
Has himself
Dried out.

Civilization!
I tell you, your perception of your own Self-Worth
Has long been dying from neglect pure;
Your soul needs Emotional Depths and Substance
And not the masked saviour you loved yesterday;
Your scattered Soul needs
Substance from words, gestures and promises
And you must no longer peep at the liar's glances
That felt free
To dance
In any motion and movement it felt;
While you stood there, consuming nothing from your insecure saviour –
You stand there alone,
Drenched by brittle dryness and desperately waiting for an unknown appointment
In a hidden destination in No Man's Land;
You stand there still waiting
Waiting for your hero's suggestions;

While your passions that explode so discretely
You then realize just how much you need
Your own Emotional Essences
Your Emotional Essence needs the bleeding to stop
Now
As you attempt to amputate your soul's troubled edges.

For all your friendless 'friends'
And their posh gatherings
And the glamorous wicked nights
Where money was nonsense
In the eyes of your Self
You still stand there alone
Thinking of the moments
Of so many years ago
Viewing your life's scenery
That you so feel for
All troubling
And adding to nothing
Nothing and going fast nowhere
Speaking words, feelings and ideas
Arguing and loving and working
Dressing your body -
But, whatever you may do
Strips you bare ever more
Strips you your scant and remote truths
That are dwindling;
Starving in your empty civilization
That is descending into a
Frozen death!

❦

The End

Goodnight
A Truth speaks
Just as She
Falls gracefully
Sweetly to
Sensible Sleep
And surrenders
Her own
Mortal Words
To Eternity
True

&

The Final Poem Man Will Write

Come then, to write your words
They, that filled
And inspired
So few

For before you
Were grounded
So many songs
Of truths
Forgotten

And now you
Write what beliefs
Exist within you
But I say this:
Folly of your minds
Shall be
The Final Poem
Man will Write.

☙❧

The Great Pretender

I was never too sure
If I was right or wrong
They were just mere abstractions to me
My mind of nothingness you wish to visit?
I loved this one
Or that one
What did I know
About all of them, I knew nothing
That was my truth
But, then, I didn't know my truths
Nor did they!
I lived roles
I breathed images
I continued to produce
Manufactured thoughts
Manufactured opinions
That I then
Believed were
To be truths
And then guess what
I defended these manufactured stones
And I became passionate
For them;
Idiot soul!
How can stones
Be passionate?
I dressed this way and more
And did talk in this style
But what was it all to mean

I thought
It meant so much!
But it meant naught really
I was a nothingness real
Living in a vivid world
Of vaguest abstractions
Wherein the end
Emptiness
Was the grand net total
Created between us all here, for now..
I went to universities
To study the philosophy of stupidities
Yes, my God, indeed!
How I never even managed to learn that much
These philosophies
Of Nothingnesses!

৪৫

The Helping Hand

When truth's smile
Begs
To begin
In her only
Life
That hurts
To breathe;

Beautiful smile
Come and cry,
On my broken
Shoulder
As I try
To live
For you.

෪෫

The Inhuman Journey

Peace; Souls, herewith are the Blessings of Certainty
Passed unto the Needy
Across agitated oceans of distances
Never part with your beliefs

Peace, Souls migrating, from lands Harsh to lands Unknown
There may be no relief in this world
Yet, tomorrow, in the skies there shall be Serenity Supreme
Press ahead, then; press ahead, in your Inhuman Journey

ঔ

The Moment of a Midnight

Well there's a smile
And I think
Of a room and its views
That laughs distantly

My hunger
Equals my sorrow
And my dreams
They meditate
And when I lie awake and alone
The colours I see are black and blue
With their shades and sisters

It is a certain hour
I know
Time betrays us
Instantly and all too soon
This night is powerful
And I am thinking
The ghosts of my past
That are so happily
Sitting by

ତ୍ରୀ

The Paranoid Logician

I'm beginning
In my
Mind
To *believe*
In a
Truth;
But Truth
Abandons me -
And so
I exist
Mindless
And alone.

꧁꧂

The Will

1995
Ayad bin Izzet

Sweetness
And when my life
Shall cease
Come then
To write
Your words
That shall give birth
To me;

Sweetness
Yes I watched
You
As you lived
So unaware
Of my paths
That I blindly
Pursued.

৪৫

This Day is to be Repeated Tomorrow

Tell it to the fields of war
'Never to be forgotten' she wrote words
Such chances reside within life
While bloodied thorns ravage senses
Exasperated in personal prisons
Truths revolving nowhere
Disconsolate landscape reflective and pensive
Creatures breathing weariness alone
Figures passing by each other without
Anyone noticing
This day is to be repeated by tomorrow
Today's twin is tomorrow
And food matters little now
As paths of lives sink within
And journeys cease and expire.

જ

This Worldly Life

Across a belief
Rides a man
Hopping on crutches
Where thorns of a Christ
Nailed his needs
Eternally
For this worldly life
And the many
Did not see him
Walk
Struggling across
To his destination of death
Finality all too soon.

&c

Those Who Were Crowned, Yet They Never Knew

When so many die
You feel
When so many perish in pain vivid yet distant
You cry
When so many noble and smiling suffocate helplessly
You think
So many, years and years, of memories within your heart
Those who were crowned, yet they never knew
Those who were praised by all virtue's gods, yet they never heard

I listen to myself, here as I stand
The times that question me so steadfastly
Who do you turn to, then, in such hours wearying
Who will understand your comradeship
The animals know full well Man's nature and they turn away
Tell me then, whoever you may be – how will stillness icy turn to laughter

Do not weep, bird
Feathered beauty of innocence fair and freedom just
Do not weep for your heart, though many question you
Though the many wish to kill you
Others, may, stand by you
Justice may embrace you, shelter you and free you to the skies above

When I am asked, why this method of existence
I reply, because, somehow, the future shall reap rewards brighter
Somehow, the future shall crown my trials
Somehow, the future shall embrace me with serenity
Somehow, the future shall surround me with six daughters
Thus, alone I stand now;
Tomorrow may yet offer me the essence of humans warm and sincere

The minds that are closed
The poverty-stricken who blame themselves
The poverty-stricken who are endlessly ashamed of themselves
What, then, do you speak unto such souls weary and tired
How, then, do you lift their burdens unfair
How do you tell them that it is they who are just in claiming what is theirs
And what, then, is their 'theirs'
Yours are the riches
Yours are the fruits of all your labour
Yours are the sweats' rewards
Yours are whatever fruition your toil has brought unto yourselves
The years of labour you have done, we say, it shall return to you
Yet, as you now look around you
All those years you have laboured
Where are your rewards accumulating
Where are your benefits that should justly comfort you beyond all frustrations
Where your children's toys
Why is your salary and wages still the same

Earth revolves as it has
Millions before you have lived, thought, loved, hated and died
Millions shall do the same in the unknown vastness of the future
Blue planet swirling the heavens celestial
How silent are the screams of millions as you exist now
Upon the soil of this revolting planet

∞

Thoughts of an Outcast

Everywhere there are people trying
To breathe
Air that is living
And breathing
That is somehow alive

Beauty lady
Heaving truths
I loved you endlessly
While you just massaged
Your thoughts
Into truths
What, then, became
Of your truths?

I saw you
You work
Paid rent
Christ
It never did happen for you
There just was no happiness
Was there?
And what could I actually do?

Sweet beauty
Sweet daughter
What could I do
If you chose
Never to listen to me?
What, then, could, I ever do for you?

They say
Some hour
A moment will come
A suddenly appearing sparrow
Will forcefully whisper upon
My battered ear
Saying
"It's time
For actual PEACE!"

Christ
I'm in need
Of it
Have I had not enough troubles, Sir?
Everywhere I see children laughing
Sir;
Give me
Some rest.
Since 1989
I've been in hurt
And horror
I think
I've paid my time
In all those years
Sir

ৰেত

Threat of Having a Panic Attack

Everywhere I lived
I was threatened
By blood that was blood in its ugly confusion
Never again
I screamed
To gods
Within me
They laughed
Telling me
We're all liars
Didn't you even guess?

I was chosen to be chased by indiscriminate hating demons
The furies of Madness
If only you stood one second in the hail
Of bullets I had to stand in front of
Then you would have appreciated or understood me
Screaming fears that seem to explode from your fleshy skull
I needed to jump out of a train
I needed to scream
I needed to run mad
Injure myself
Hoping the shock would kill Panic
Yes, it is called 'panic' by the way

But I couldn't really quite discuss it
Peacefully & calmly could I?
Then you would have feared me
Wouldn't you?
And besides what good what I achieve by telling anyone
Of my ills?

My own psychiatrists are worse off than me
In their stench-full mixtures of stupidities & arrogance
Asking me, with acute boredom, pointless questions
While I was fearing for my sanity

Death to Psychiatry and Psychiatrists!

ဆေ

To Quantify Hurt

I think I gave much
I made mistakes but my heart was
Concerned for her
Though she was different from me
We got nothing between us
She was south
I was north
Nothing joined with
Nothing
She said "Greetings!"
I heard "Goodbye!"
Hatreds grew
And purity faded
Scared scarred faces
Hiding
Behind
Veils of indecency
How immeasurable
Do sins hurt
Children
Yes I know
I cannot count
What hurt means
To a
Child
Quantify hurt
And you yield tears
That turns into
Anger
And soon
Just maybe
They turn into
Revenge
A man thinks endlessly trying to find truth
I tell him
You're being just too late
Truth
Passed away a just
A Few
Centuries ago from your
Hamlet here.

ॐ

Too Late

So children
Come to listen
To my early words
Of a sudden sorrow
That warned of the echoes
That shall come for certain
My words, I guess decided
To escape from you,
All of you
Who now decide to look
Inside myself

And if one
Were to speak out
Their only pronouncements
And asked me
I would have so gladly defended
You all
And I would then have
Never disappointed you!
For your sanity, I knew
Was so much in the balance
Since no one could ever
Be dividing my brain;
I just wish you had called out
For me
In time
To help you so.

✶

Tortures of Every Twist Imaginable

Silently
Graves tell you of
Their individual stories
Each one of them
Has a special story
To tell
Can you be Patient enough to listen
And actually absorb?

Millions before us all
Have Suffered
Endless and pointless
Tortures
Of every twist imaginable
Due to the ugly human brain

Christ!
Some of us here, down here do need Help
And not just psychiatrists' eternally
Pointless sighs
Of boredom
We must pay for.

જી

Troubled Child

So listen then
Here
To a word
I passed by
An hour ago
When a child
Of angelic eyes
Spoke to me
With a wandering and vague face
And wisdom teeth
Like pearly grains of sand;
She moaned of the ills
To be done
By others and herself;
Beautiful girl
Standing there so straight
Am I your mirror
You seek to reflect from?

∽

Truth? What 'Truth' Do You Speak Of?

In some moments her Eyes Flippant at times can look
At times staring bloodily
I see Her
Solemn hideous grimaces
That are supposed to tell me what?
Her minds swears, for she has proclaimed
Her 'Proclamation of Truth!'
You, there – anyone, everyone must hear
Feelings are no longer enough for her
Discard all your thoughts, for now you will hear what the Gods themselves have to Say

She speaks: "And, yes your wealth can at times make you feel aghast at yourselves,"
"Deny your every viewpoint, and then you shall feel the strength,"
"Destroy all your previous songs, ideas, passions and loves,"
"For now, the days triumphant, are emerging,"
"O alas *Ye* old ones!"
"Alas! Alas! Do not Despair!"
"Tell me, you wise ones who anointed yourselves so,"
"What do your thoughts and emotions add up to?"
"Remember that everything you did, was repeated before,"
"Every memory you have loved and hated, has been experienced before,"
"Every event you have enjoyed and hated, has been played out before,"
"So what is unique unto you, then?"
"What do you think makes you so meaningful, then?"
She then ceased to Speak
Tell me, O do tell me, I yearned for more!
Again and again, I needed her
Her voice disrupted and discontented me
As I understood that no 'Truth' can exist
Without its contradictions
Terminating it.

☙❧

Truths and Their Consequences

If an empty bowl or plate appeals for itself
Appeals for food
If a desperate moment cries its needs for hopeful songs
They, that are so
Needing sustenance
And all they get
Are mumbled slogans
That revolves dizzily
Vomitingly towards plasticity
And if a suspicious hand shaking
Aches for meaningful humanity's touch
And if a genuine smile tells you a sincere lie
And if a curse comes to teach you to hope for a brighter tomorrow
Where will you then stand, when you think of all Truths?
Who will you converse with in a meaningful manner?
And Truths suffer
They suffer sincerely from
Cultures of stupidity
Cultures of brain damaging
Silliness
Cultures of apathy
Cultures needing boredom
And cultures feeding from boredom
And some sing words of meanings
Some speak words of relevance
Yet curtains rise and the actors so often see an empty applauding audience
Your culture is draining people's sanity
These are the truths and their consequences.

෨෪

Truths Shall Not Render You to Weep

Unto those who reflect upon the mute sublime
Those who Inspire the sorrowful to hope, despite their passionate dew drops
Do you not feel those who Corner their minds with the significantly vile?
Tell the worthy ones of praises gentle
Tell the frightened ones of heights loving
Where temperatures maintained your dignity
Where beauty disguised your horror
Your instances that must be momentary
So do not weep for them, as so many do
This is not at all profound, do you not think so?
Misunderstood Hatreds that can be frustrating are speaking in you
Trying to explain the rationality of their origins
As the errors of your existence are still being spelled incoherently
Tell us, great mother, and great leader, unto you we choose to follow
Your followers died starving in their angers burning, despite your appeals for success
Whatever happened to the calm that appeared questioning that rancid storm?
What rage changed your colours hourly?
You all
Everywhere
Of all times
Where do you hear me?
Tell me, where do you stand?
When we know what repulsive deeds Man does do
How much can I give?
How much can I feel?
How much can I hate?
The savvy lynchers
How many can I defend?
The fragments of mistakes do speak to me
Alone as I sit here
How long can we stand?
How long can you keep that smile of life and soul and happiness?
My soul, quivers down my fragmenting spine endless
That speaks
Of the Lords of yours
That Scream to the soulless inhumanity that abandons you
Forsaken child, do not weep;
Though life must kill you
The truths shall not render you to weep
Let hearts become bountiful in essences loving
Eyes of gods
Voices of stilted dignity
Rise up, and listen to your priorities justified

ळ

Trying to Make a Woman Understand Herself

Woman
Of a fluid eye
That cannot believe in herself
Never mind your mistakes
Never mind your stupidities
History is immoral
Why do you insist on hurting yourself
When you will inevitably die anyway?
And lying now
In some random bed
You are deceiving and hurting
Your unknown selves
And who will care for you
For you will suffer
And decay
Woman!
You loved
But who can even remember you now
Tonight
Such are laws
Mechanical and cold, universal
Laws of life, physical
Existing to expand
Capital
Listen to your words
The disconnected words you use
The dysfunctional thoughts you use
In your handwriting
In your lives
All of you
Are sorrowful
Don't you even
Know?

⭗

Trying to Speak

I love you
Child
Of mine
I can only love
This much
Before my finality appears
I am losing
My soul's Mind
Here within, hidden from you all;
I am trying
To speak sense
While frantically fearing my Self
So, listen then, listen
You, who feel it only too worthy
To refuse my words -
Where then
Can I ever go
Now
I am nowhere
In my earthly life

&

Trying to Understand Answers

I called for Peace & Humanity
But I saw filth of culture, human mud & burned faces
I saw people eating fried flesh
I saw babies mature as crucified slabs of meat
Strange I guessed
So this is where we are at?
I saw a prostitute
Hungry for work
I asked her: "Woman! What are you doing?"
"Wisdom is money & money is wisdom" she replied hoarsely
I understood
She was far too exhausted to understand anyone else
I saw a gambler and I asked him:
"Man! Why do you so obsessively gamble"
And he said: "I'll gamble all my money, because I must."
I said to him: "But you'll bankrupt you're family."
He said to me in a thirsty voice:
"I need to if I am to be fabulously rich."
I stared at him puzzled.
"I'm thirsty too", he continued,
"But my thirst is different
"From your hunger."
And I understood he finished his speech.

Soon I saw a murderer
Who laughed at his joy
"Man! What are you doing?" I asked him seriously
He laughed back, "Go to your cot, fool!"
He squeaked
"Is that your rightful answer?" I asked
"Yes, what more did you need?" he replied like a humble worm
"If I don't butcher, I'll be butchered!"

And soon I saw a dying child
Painting a painting I understood not
"Child! What do you do and why?" I asked
He was too feeble to explain
I couldn't tell if his sombre eyes
Were gazing at me, or staring weakly
Or wether they were even noticing me at all.

And I saw a widow with several young children
"Why are you in this grievous situation widowed one?"

She smiled uncomfortably
"I was fooled into marriage; I was deserted by my
Savage husband."
"So you are not a 'widow' then?" I asked.
"Well, he killed himself later, you see."
"But why did he steal away his own life?" I asked.
"You think I care?
"I have enough worries just surviving, Sir."
I understood not and walked on.

Soon, I met a Prophet.
"Sire, what's going on with all these sorrowful Humans?" I asked.
The Prophet looked at me bored
"Humans are Fools, so why do you ask a foolish question?"
Then, I walked on towards a destination
I simply did not care about
As per its
Directions.

৪৩

Twisted Dog

A dog was alone
In coldness
Wild
Where stones wept
And blood
Dried.

Never in bitterness' History
Did Coldness marry
Hatred
So defined.

Shallow reactions
Followed
A law that
Fruitlessly dawned.

And
A dog did cry
Voice twisted
And chained alone;
Why?
For he was found
To
Having befriended Man.

୧୨

Twists of Your Ugliness

And if a human
Speaks to you
What twists do you feel?
Tell him your needs, and laugh
Hate him
The moment cannot be worth it
In the end
Dictate boredom
Dictate boredom to the boring
Till they see
And if a Human speaks to you
Laugh, because nothing can mean
Especially 'love'
Concepts you love
For the truths bear naught to your concepts
Your face
Its twists
Its ugliness
Yes, ugliness undefined
Understand
What dark concepts seduce you?
Understand the hollowness of your borrowed tunes
Understand the momentariness of your needs
Understand the weakness of yourselves.

&

Tyrant

Only at Freedom's Death
Do you now talk
Of your hurt's truths,
Burned by an oily anger
Raging at your world

As I sit to think
From the errors of your past
I wrote words of remembrance
For all seasons true

The pained blood
Of ancient Scriptures
That pleaded with you
Just so to listen
Once and only for once
To this saddening chapter
We now call the sorrowful Twentieth Century

In its final gasp
And it still screams out
Her maimed groans
For no Man could yet
Be alive
In this prison
You called my Nationhood

O how could you then
Mutilate
Sacred Souls
So much wiser than you
As they dreamed
In their endless attempts
To convince you
Of their passion's love

And still
All these truths
Were but footnotes
In your murderous life.

೧೦

Unbalanced Woman Scribbling Her Thoughts

Who was thinking
When I was myself
Trying to
Figure out
What
And who I am

But I know and I knew always that I myself
And my own mind were
Far too thoughtless
To realize anything

Because I owned
Or I was possessed by
Far too many blobs
Of inertia
In my empty spaces
That I think
Resided in my brain

And they, I agree, did appear
Just far too many times
For my stability
And my comfort
For too many times they appeared
In my thinking, breathing, feeling, loving

Oh! Are you surprised
That I, the fool, to you
Am still capable of 'feelings' and 'love'?!
Well, I do
But, I do accept that no one
From your world of stability
And serenity
Can have 'feelings' for me

I was dying
I knew
But I decided to ask this
Question angrily
Because that is all you
Balanced humans tell me

So, I chose to ask you
I did decide that
I will and shall
Ask you
All

What is 'dying' and all that?
You people keep talking about
When you happen to pass by me?

You always politely answer
To my Self
Your explanations
To my female universe
That inhabits my observing mind

"It all begins with you getting
Away from this life
And your society and all that."
You professionals 'preach' or 'speak' to me
I confuse between those and these
Two
Excuse me

Guess what?
I replied
To those ever changing scientists
Psychiatrists and counsellors
And psychologists and
I'm getting bored with all
Yourself crowned
Labels you stick on your daft heads

Yes, I'm talking about you artists, geniuses
And doctors and hospital workers
And to humans
Feeling awkward
When they are walking and passing me by in the streets
Or, just wait
Maybe, it is that I am
The one who is
Passing by them?

So I speak and preach to you too!
Listen here, to my whatever passions:
I'm already a hermit

I'm already a recluse
From all of you Humans

So I guess I'm already
Dead
In your far away minds
I guess so, no?

People, humans, spoke and mumbled
To God knows who
All together
They communicated;
But
I chose
To walk
Far away.

&

Unity

You live for now
This life
That has
Begun
To hate
You
In me
I stand
In my early times
Running for a forgiveness
Scattered hopes
Loving touches
From a soul
You may now love
They deny you
You rise
You cry
You plead, sweet one
They are so determined
In their obsessions
To kill
From a tomb
Of love
To a cradle
Of tears
You write
Your fragmented alphabets
My only friend
I write to you
Though we've been separated
Can we only now begin to live
In this life
I ask you
I tell you
Let us all be one.

୧୦

Unknown Saviour

Where can you be found
Now you are
Lost
In a land
Of such unbelieving
Souls
Searching in fear
For their
Unknown Saviour
Who stands
So right besides
You all.

෨෨

Unknown Soldier

You tried to whisper words in a scream
That all came forth far too convoluted
Doom's clouds raining fierce
Against the luxuries of those who dream
This is indeed
A terror to gasp – A tale to tell
Of far too great dimensions
Oh! Emotional contradictions wearying supreme
You tried to cry; you tried to voice responsible ideas –
But you were met with pupils in trances aloud:
Entities too proud
To admit shame, defeat and grief
Entities to proud to weep.

Soul, laden with beauty, transformed into a reckless recluse –
With a gasping audience of universal fools
So drugged and self-abused
Tell me Why?
You didn't hear the news
On the stabbing of Jesus in His hour of gloom?
Do you think History has relevance to us all, or not?
Unknown Soldier!
Your tale, the careless winds have drifted them away;
And generations are none the Wiser, my dears
For all of our done pained deeds
We all turn away – for wherever a limp light may flicker
Unknown Soldier!
With a proud Mother and your bland, simple name
A childhood; a cosy love and a thousand memories more
Your treasures fell with you – secrets and all
Unknowing characters spoiled and tainted your pride
Providing you with even further Pain
While you gaze at this earth and her History
From your simple trenches
And it is all Passing by you
Oblivious
And carrying no shame nor any morality
Unknown Soldier!
Unknown as you are and unknown you shall for Eternity be:
Though they counsel you, "They Shall Not Be Forgotten!"
I do wonder, What minds taught you throughout your life?
From behind their tattered veils?
Unknown Soldier!

Unknown as you are –
Your pride pushes you to serve on
But, Should it, too, fall some moment,
I hope it Will never turn to dust
No! And a thousand years or more
May pass;
Throughout which, a million human clowns in wandering disgrace
Will live out their merry lives
Your Dignity remained;
Forever shall remain
A symbol, a painted canvas of colours, literature and music;
Forever a burden for all my lameness
Forever etched, carved and inscribed
In my brain
For masses to witness

Though you remained in your briefest of life forever tormented
By the most insignificant
Haunted by the smirking insane
Didn't they tempt your insecure strengths?
And threatened your fulsome stability aloud?
O Unknown forgotten fool and a bore
Collapsed in your once great might
And became such a forgotten wind of brevity;
Your mask, eternal, piercing and true;
Will sit there abused, sickly and aloof –
All can and will laugh again or more –
For you are no burden unto anyone

Your Existence, once so stubborn, is now speck of dust
For all the wicked masses who may wish to see:
And for what exactly?
For Ancient and Modern History?
Monument that you are –
You perished amidst the yawning spectators, my dead friend
Your physicality has long since been scattered
In its trivial remains
Amidst the condescending living ones
Across the ages
O! Unknown Soldier!
Having dispensed with your life's pleasures, worthy and real
So wretchedly
Agonizing, as you did
For so long a days;
Why despair and bury your Ugly Self now
So miserably?
Do you regret your service now?
As you review and witness your decades and years
Questioning what worth it contained therein
No! My man;
For treasures of any entity are not to be clung to and kept
And this is my gentle wisdom unto you
May you now Translate it into a thousand languages and their feelings;
And by the grace of endurance, will and a knowledge
Of certainty
You may feel peace
For such is Victory Immortal
To be forever and eternally
True.

&

Vile 'Human'

An evening wherein I find sitting
Supper's Traitor sitting gleeful next to me
And so Begins the eerie moment
That I feel
Seeks to wilfully extinguish
A life's fragile candle.

The incomprehensible scenes I see
In my silent eyes
Seemingly never ending
Wild expanses
Visions of Hurt, Sorrow and Loneliness
That I cannot understand, define or explain.

Seeking any role to play
We turned for comfort
To any random guiding and guided Fool
Look at the utter beauty of the liars
Around us all
Spelling mistakes they make, though we heard poetry
That seriously changed our brief lives.

But we mustn't lie about our mistakes
Let us listen to our deathly end's opening night
Coming so soon
A majestic Silence and Symphony
For all our final moments
To ponder about.

And are we still acting, we, the despised 'human'
Acting beyond reason and its compassion
My God
We shall soon meet you
And how will we then react?

Ancient victim,
Still writing
Your romantic scripts for senseless lovers
I will tell you
Do not accept or forgive the glamorous Remorse of Judas
Seek his annihilation, without a breath of mercy

Forsaken children,
Abandoned by the vilest parent creatures Man has known
Tears of your Farewell
That will soon be Forgotten
Are screaming still
So think just how
Awfully pointless they all are.

ಲಿ

Victims Seeking Hope

Excuse the facts
They lie to themselves
Standing lonely and alone
As I stood there crying

Child aghast!
Where were your childhood plans
In your safest hours?
Tell the children
Drowned and beaten blue
Our tales melt in your lives routine;
My sorrow walks from a fading Smile
And my Smile is a tender crucifix
Painted and merged on your face

Everywhere people seeking avenues and paths
Money is your problem
Rent is your problem
Friendship is your problem
Fear is your problem
Dragging you inside and nowhere
We do not know ourselves, I say
In ourselves, Nothing
Do we know
Nothing do we care
Nothing, do we feel
So, admit it all
And lie on.

&

Visions Beheld by Youth, Once

Visions beheld by Youth, once
Are by now
Ancient dimmed memories now
For other times may so be alive
Remember your shaken prejudice and hatreds
In your innermost turmoil

In joy, maidens and soldiers lived a delightful life
While God chose to chop you into slices of sorrow
Why did you not believe in the strengths of your life?
Why did you not embrace an ideology of Strength?
A love cannot be – Forget 'Love' I tell you!
Whistling mad-men compose fiction and non-fiction books
Hoping to proclaim Liberty's positive paths for all humans to relate to
Grand, monumental structures were but a testimony to Man's hatred of Man
And for Man's sincere deification of himself
So seek the ruthless Annihilation of all who are harmful
And I, one citizen, stern and sorrowful
Deceived by regret I cannot believe in no more
Such an age's pronouncements I now reject categorically
Seek to Stitch your wounds of innocence
Seek to properly Doom mad-men's prophesies that claim to cure
For they only seek to Burn dead your fragile brains
Upon the well-known crucifixes made from the of sickest flesh of humans
Whilst gentle dwarfs, in such steps
To tunes of harmony grotesque
Marched forth ever more to crematories; alive and welcome
They were to be; for they so sinned against the irreverent gods
And so they had to be Burned
As the sickly aristocratic fools live out their lives in perpetual boredom
Will
Calm return?

These, then
Were the
Visions beheld by Youth once
Utterances of gladness
Forever to be;
Much too many
Souls have been spent
Much too many
Souls, like you and I
Have been
Forever more gone

ᛣᛉ

Wanderer

For my love
I needed
A bone
To discover
My ancient smile.

⚭

Wasted Lives

Come here
Lost children
Upon the fields
Of forgetfulness
I tell you
All your poppies
Alive and unreal
Will be forgotten
In Time
Soon;
So, come here
Wandering children
There's a road
Speaking to you
Of its future and needs
So tell your children
Upon their awakening
Of certain misfortunes
And hardships sure
Ahead.

જ્

Wave a Last Farewell

I saw twenty horses seriously ache for pity's nourishment
In wilderness' roads that perpetually laugh and lie unto travellers
The despairing ears of a deaf soul imagined uselessly
What language and tone can possibly mean
The dust filled eyes of a blind jester wept blackness sore
The two conversing humans lying to one another
I felt that
They groped for their arguments only
A woman demanding Reason stood still naked and alone
Fearing for her sovereignty
Just as too many chained children were depressed and walking
This world was ineligible, I wrote throughout my life
"Take us away from this freedom! I heard citizens of 1789 and 1917 opine
I see the Blurred orphans chant faintly from distances foggy
For 'Decency'
Which soon prompted
The roars of the many shocked hungry ones and made the few
Laugh in pleasant smiles
The cries of the angry were not echoed meaningfully
By the dull 'forces' of Justice
The wealthy dined on buttery blood well-hidden and disguised with grease and cream
No one really knew
How the chefs cooked up such dishes
This world
Your world
Can be too filling

For those whose bellies reek with emptiness
Where else could you go
You wished
The festivities and pomp all would die
So you can have a measly morsel or two
And then we must think aloud
When we realise that what we need
Is not and will never be there for us
The circles of life continue
As repetitions
We've seen it before
The names may change
The faces change
Sceneries change
But the patterns remain steadfast
Monuments ancient with wisdom rot
To extinction
And none will worry
None will understand
Wave a farewell to life's mixtures
The abstract and the 'real'
Wave a last farewell
If you can!

☙❧

We Are All Fare Too Insignificant

People that you happily butcher
Unearthed, unceremoniously dug up by pleasant archaeologists
Exhumed from any dignity they may have had
From dusty, tearful memories
Broken fragile remains
Now, given your infinitely vast crimes
And what you've committed before and forever more
I stand lame, bland and pathetic
While you laugh joyfully
At the History you so proudly create.

Unheard of burdened orphans
Seeking some minds pure, sincere
That needs love
And affection
We will crawl with due submission
For a thousand unpleasant miles
Just to reach you
And, yes, maybe, we may just realize
Our needs
Or maybe it was
All in our blackest of dreams.

We are the hungry ones, I proclaim!

The ones, you never heard of
Hungry and sorrowful
My beloved
Misunderstanding never ceases
Because, we are all
Far, far too insignificant

And, it's all as simple as that
I'm just all too
Insignificant
And we are all
Far too insignificant.

৩৫

We Are All Prisoners in This Life

Ruined, filthy room, despite your brave cleansing attempts
Messengers mentioned and whispered and hinted where the escape keys may be
Cautiously the feelings of prophets and the self proclaimed prophets
Preach their manuscripts on how to achieve freedom
Silently, I heard a shy, insecure tune that was meant to soothe your nerves
The crazed smiles of a common lunatic expressed momentary sincerity
Followed by the most rigid, faulty shallowness
While solemn, pompous psychiatrist men and woman insisted on continuing their talks
For no reasons that I personally understood
And we all wished them a speedy end
For they lavishly created uncertainties and fears
And lots of cash, too!

The terribly bored skies were beginning to randomly mock us
In everything between our insides hidden
The couple of bored lovers played
The prescribed game for them, again and again
Ad nauseam
While a severely overweight clown with
Mascara and greedy sweat heavily mingling
Suddenly begat to laugh so hysterically
At himself and at everyone else
Why, I really thought he was going fall from his feet.

Smoking cannot be good, twenty serious thinkers thought
And they thought really hard
At that proposition
Thinking that humans would be interested
To hear what thoughts they were thinking about
Yet, but when did anything – like thoughts or thinking - matter to bored humans?
You must have guessed some of the god's
Worthless tricks being played upon us!

And blessed are the sincere liars, for they do materially so well in life
Life that is presumed to be filled with truths, love, compassion and humanity
The innocent ones wept, for they were hurt you know by
Their blatant inability to act the required roles!
Now you must have felt humanity's pinch, I wondered for these hurt ones?
And to the astonishment of all:
Nobody really felt anything for the innocent ones.

The times spoke ancient tales for the ready-made and pre-packaged human beings
If you do believe in life so much, you may well die for its gruesome offensiveness

Crying for the blood of the blinded and handcuffed one who did naught
"Go die, I screamed in my wisdom forlorn, for we are all prisoners here!"

What use and benefits did the venerable senators and congressmen do for you all?
If you love the Mortuary Men,
Then what else can you expect from them?
Life! – Are you that stupid!?

The intense experiences you think of, were all fake
All the times you presumed were truthful, loving and passionate were insincere
Kill those memories of infectious trash, and they'll tell you soon
The roads of life are vaguely manifold, you must have known
So feel the Skin of your Soul, here and now;
And live for no other purpose
The ones who sigh, know it all.

The loving trees and their adoring branches were amputated yesterday
By conservationists seeking votes;
And yes, we dutifully applauded praised the times for its truths and sincerities
All the time, I was alone
Desperately trying to gather my Self, here and nowhere
Yet between it all, I swear my dysfunctional, distant heart did say so:
Saying scornful messages to me;
Within our wearied Soul, across the breathtaking boundaries of time and space
I felt I needed to laugh
As soon as I feel I am in the Heavenly Skies
The Skies we shall all so soon beautifully share in harmony pure!

ॐ

Welcome Me in Your Lives

Welcome me into your lives
Welcome me into your minds
Those that rejected
My life
And her soul
Because
Because it is so inhumanly cold
This sickening
Dawn
It burns with a freezing
Hatred
Lashing out at my terrified smile
That tries
Just to survive
In this bewildering world
That you all create
Welcome me
Please
In this invisible life
Of yours
Where polite protocol
Means more than the needs of poverty
Where irrelevant conversations
Mean more than starving insecurities
Please
Welcome me
Somewhere
Because I am now
Trying to run
From my self
That has so much
Failed me.

ରଓ

Welcome to the Carnival of Humanity!

Welcome to the Carnival of Humanity!
Welcome to the Carnival
Of Indiscriminate Torture practiced by pleasant eyes
Come with whatever your own eyes you may have
As you watch the gaudy scenes
That we'll arrange for you
Watch and relax
Take down notes, if you desire.
Write what you feel
And feel out what you wish to write
For this is our Theatre of Democracy
I think you will understand us
And you may even laugh along with us
All of us here are a part of You
Crammed in our mutual bureaucracy
In our jumbled, incoherent offices.

You may paint your faces
Any emotion you desire or fake
You may paint our morbid hearts
You may laud our 'Humanity'
That meanders and laughs at its impotence
We can make you laugh, I tell you
In this Happy Show
We'll make you smile beyond your reflexes.
You see, just as the tortured ones
Were victims of their own misguided words
And just as the elites were stock-holders
In the game of gambling
That we respectfully call 'Capitalism'
In the end, really, who were the crooks?

Gaze at that righteous Syrian belly dancer
Who seeks to Tempt the hermit philosophers
In the hope she will shape their desires
But instead, they proceeded to wage wars;
You see houses being bombed
You see mothers scream
You witness the endless nights
The mutilating rockets and their fame
See the 'friendships' melt away
See how 'friends' turn to their self-interest
See the poverty and the hunger of minds
See the mother who sold what she had
So please don't talk to me about love, peace and harmony
Because we do not care anymore
No one cares for anyone
We are all humans living in a world of Chance
Sprinkled with a dash of our Guesses and their humble Memories
That eventually burn themselves into Nothingness
Are we distorting ourselves and the truth?
Does our carnival and our intentions mean naught to you?
Yes, perhaps indeed
Especially when you do consider that
All is nothing.

୬୧

Welcome to the World

In between hatred and love
An abandoned child hungered for truth
Hurt and burned beyond recognition
Deformed by the mass slaughter
Of a casual maniacal ruler
Who seriously preached words of restraint
And optimistic caution
I'm wondering where you all came from
Dear friends
Children
Being
Turned over to lightly painted
Pimps
Who laughed uproariously
And danced
To see their stolen flesh being burned
And see them licking the dripping fat
From the scarred innocence of the sacrificed
Beauties
Who never did get to understand
The meanings
Of one hateful hating bullet
That was intensely, intentionally directed
At the appalled deaf, dumb and blind lambs
Who were shrieking noises and who were running
Hither and thither
Son and girl
Listen to my words
If you want
Endless chants of peace will achieve nothing
For the cries of the jailed living martyr
In solitary Confinement
Cannot ever express to you their hurt
While, outside, see those endless glamorous Fraudsters
Playing the ever changing roles of 'lovers'
And playing the roles of 'preachers'
They're all decomposing
That's how I see it
My evenings are dark
Where hopelessness
Does overwhelm the oceanic majority of humankind

&

What a Pointless Life

You know I never did live
My life
My Life

I lied all my life
All these days
Pointless conversations
That were passionate
Emptying days
Leading to my appointed
Final day
What a thankless life
Did I go through
And thank you
To whomsoever gave it all to me!

❧

What Did You Come Here For?

I have tried to speak
And overcome the pleasures of stupidities
Gentlemen! Gentlemen!
What did you come here for, then?
If not to surprise yourselves with empty laughter?
Come now! I say
Do not regret what has died!
I am now here before you
Question what you can
And question who you can
For this will not last long for you
I have tried to speak
In the compassionate name of History
The screeching and the melodic that are combined
Did you listen?
Or read?
Or hear?
Or see?
Or feel?
Or understand?
So what then, is the use here
For me
To speak?

෨෧

What Did You Feel Dad?

Daddy
Where are you tonight
Dad you feared Death so much
And tonight
You're dead
So where are you
Touch me
Tell me
Sir
Are you in Heaven?
Do you see the wandering
Ghosts of Heaven?
I'm feeling pain
Daddy
What did you feel during those hours?
Of the operation
Did you
Feel it was your
End
Sir?
How frightened where you?

&

What Difference Does It Make?

Waiting
And Time, remains waiting for you
Asking you to understand it
Sorrow's gowns have been disrobed
The figure of flesh expresses itself being naked
Some exist expecting to be embalmed
Others to be destroyed forever

Sad of the Earth!
I call upon thee all to awaken
And understand the meanings
Of your plight's trails
And your forgotten lives
For existence is struggle,
And it is a spiteful struggle
Within anger everywhere brooding, festering
In directions aimed at anyone

Kill the pompous
The oppressors
The self-pitying professional fools
Look at those idle mansions
And the casually squandered riches

And I see a new religion shall be heralded
That I do see
Passionate communalism ethical and warm, it shall all be
Where else can life wander to?
Ask yourselves these words unto your selves, I ask you
Hate the liars and the self-hating and the vain and the extravagant ones
See the colours of life scattered
Know the art of mixing colours
Know the art of juxtaposing colours
Know the art of ideas presented by the holy righteous
Humanistic ones
Thus is life and its plentiful twists

For colours are themselves your emotions
And it is up to you to envision these feelings
And their practical uses to you in your daily life
These words are written
For you to understand the harmony and the necessity of contradictions
The changing twists of emotions and their abstract sources

That are indefinable
No heaven shall save thee while you live on your earth
No choir, no opera shall rescue you
No saviour shall understand thee all
No martyr shall love you
No lover shall even think about you
No genius will ever comprehend your simplest formula
Only you
Will feel your entirety

The starting point of the foundation of one's existence
Is you being alone
As any nation stands alone
And in need of alliances and allies
Build therefrom
Build the tombs for your beliefs
Build the cathedrals for revolutionaries who are bloodied
Ye children of the sleepless nights
Awaken yourselves unto a reality that is more profound
Understand the criminals that swarm around you and within
Understand the masked atheistic priests who perpetually smile
Relate to the animals that wilfully ignore your existence

Think of your pitiful dreams
And your significant needs and what they mean to you
No one will care
I tell you
Life is the process of any Twilight
The existence of your autumn is arriving fast
The farewell cards and the farewell parties are not necessary
The eulogies and lies are for what?
For your body, mind and soul
That never found any peace amidst there endless
Pathetic civil war?
Do you know perhaps see
The face of death yawning at your puzzled face
Love death, expect death with passion

Do you look stupid?
Do you feel ugly?
Can you face that feeling?
Are you as ugly as embarrassment will take you?
Are you boring?
Are you an unwanted unit?
Are you aware of these condemnations of yourself?

Will you shrivel inside?
Is this your strength?
Is this the weight of your total bravery?
How much do you hate yourself and how much do you love yourself?
Do you want to know?
How much do you needs lovers to comfort you?

The truth is
Life cares naught for you
Humans care nothing for you
What does it matter if you were alive or not?
Wether you are a fierce soul and seemingly everlasting
And wether you have children multiplying
Your personal history
Transcends absolutely nothing
Remember that fact
And try to evolve your life
Therefrom.

ဆ

What Exactly Does Matter?

The windy night decays
Along the path
Of the never to be remembered soldier
Who died recently
Amongst ten thousand others
Forgotten and laughed at

Reading literature of battles
Between rigid science and anarchic poetry
Who do you think stands to lose in their lives?
Do you think Lover will succeed in their lives?
Who Twisted the thorns of anguish inside Jesus' saintly blood?
Who Deceives their 'parents' and 'friends' and themselves from one moment to another?
If you understand
Deliver us, then, my dear one
If you can read
From the shacks and rooms of desperation
From the empty hours being spent
For cash that never will be given to you, no matter how hard you toil
It is all for nothing
But, you see, It doesn't really matter
Nothing will matter, in your and, really
Wether or not these words are being written or not
Felt and heard
Though undeciphered they may remain
In the truth
Nothing really matters much.

ꙮ

What Exactly is Life?

Life is hurtful twists
Life is meaningless struggles
Life is pointless, wretched
Life is pain beyond belief
If you can understand and feel and accept
Within yourself
Life is screaming tragedy
Life is solitary confinement, loneliness
Life is unfair in its black humour
Life is injustice against the holiest Saints
Life is discriminatory against the meek just
Life is deceiving, hypocritical and back stabbing
Life is friendless and loveless
Life is poverty, deception and oceans of human lies
Life is sickness, gangrene and cancerous paralysis
Ultimately life is fatal my friendless friends
And therein lies an essence of life itself
The fatality of life
The certainty of death that life necessarily brings upon itself
Reveals unto us a bleak meaning
That life in itself means nothing
Save a passing of the horrifying days and meaningless emotions and bland years
It is death that is the meaningful context
That gives life value
Death is the relief
Death is the passage, the gateway to freedom, to comfort
To serenity blissful, eternal
Therefore mock this life with all that you can do
Laugh bitterly at this life
Just as life laughs so venomously at the struggling, helpless pity that is you
For life is your enemy
Life is your curse; Life is your perpetual rapist
Life is your living, daily earthly hell
And death is your heaven!

∞

What is Love to You?

If I could trust
I would love
But love is beyond me
Far beyond me
Because no human has faith
So how can I trust anyone?
You speak of friendship, then
But I cannot
My friendless friend
For all your sayings
And deeds
Where did you last lie?
Your existence
Is it not manufactured?
By flippant needs
And that is what you call 'love'
What you call love
I call changing needs.

୬୧

What is the Value of Life?

Where a voice had naught to say
What did it speak?
Where is anybody
There's no one here
It's quiet here
Stunned by the moment
What do you say?
Whom do you speak to?
The people out there vague
Criticize you
Inevitably will do so
Their prejudices are confirmed
So, alone, you turn unto yourself
What am I?
What constitutes my Self?
I question my Self
Forced, as I am
I am an animal social
I am an animal adventurous
I seek knowledge
I seek meaning and patter
Yet, existence here disagrees
Existence here is moulded differently
Architecture of loneliness
An economic system of lust
Negating warmth human personal
A mass media that exalts idiocy and denigrates elevation sublime
Who am I?
I am trying to overcome my circumstances
I am trying to overcome my situation present
Child of nowhere
Child of sorrow
Passions cannot be dismissed
This is the 'life' we are being offered

This is it
Bleak existence
Education boring
Job oppressive
Existence is old age living
This is life
An existence of alliances and greed
An existence of flirting and deceiving
An existence of temporary chemical-induced euphoria
An existence of self-denial
An existence of endless empty handshakes
An existence of barren smiles forced by the situations' protocol
An existence of exasperating routine
And the future
Is the same
How odd
How predictable
Our future is so obvious
That is the tragedy of truth
Our lives are predetermined
The much feared future is known
How do I escape from that?
I saw a woman I cherished
I failed to ask her anything
Improper I thought
I ignored her
I never saw her again
I knew she liked me
Therein is the value of life

ॐ

What's Panic?

I think
God
I've had enough
Don't you think
My punishment
Should now actually end?
Sir?
Fear
Who can understand that?
PANIC
Who can comprehend that
Drunk and I can write about it
But sober I cannot
Terror
These are words
Letters
F- E- A- R
Nothing but concepts
Ideas
But panic is the worst
For anyone interested to listen.
I was in a train
I wanted to open the door
I wanted to hurl myself outside
I wanted to blow myself
Into pieces

Anything is better than
Being in & within panic
Death is greater
Than panic
I don't know how long panic lasts
I don't know where panic will take me
And no one knows
Around me
How can you tell anyone of panic?
They'll think you're evil or violent
So you remain quiet
So let's go back to panic
What is it?
It's like being thrown out from the Eiffel Tower with no parachute
It's like having your testicles being sliced off very very very gently
It's like having your eyeball gouged out very very very gently
It's like feeling that you are going to throw yourself
Out in front of an Oncoming car

෨෬

When Elegance Weeps

Soul I Love
Candle Flickers;
And Night
Tender
Yawns.

Life's Loves!
Meanings Recede;
And Elegance
I Hear
Weeps.

৪৩

When Panic Attacks You in the Midst of Night

Dreaded night
The Fear
May come
And then
Abruptly it does appear
Drenching your soul and skin with frenzied chaos
Fear that threatens
To make you kill
Your fragmenting Self
Simple, uncontrolled thoughts
Terrifies you
You slide into losing your 'self'
A violent blackness divides your unified Mind
Into screaming frenzied mutually hating
Emotionally unstable
Splinters that actively
Seek to terrify you into total mental meltdown
But it may cease
It may end
This Unholy early Hour
In this Unholy Black Night
An end may come
But the Fear stops you from
Hoping and trying to feel safe
Baby girl
Your terror
Only you and your petrified self will ever get to know
No words, no paintings
No poems, no warmth, no love
No comforts, no money, nothing will ease your mind
Until Panic itself
Decides to leave your succumbing mind
No talk can make anyone understand you
Nothing can help you
In these frantic eternal moments

So forget it
And look on yourself
Instead of trying to make
Others 'understand'
This night may end
And peace may come
Serenity may come
From within this bottomless fear
That has no words, images or colours
A peace may come
Some dawn
So soon
Baby
May be
Listen quietly, then
And endure this Night's attack, and
Wait for whatever the outcome may turn out to be

‍ॐ

When Will Peace of Mind Come?

And in some moments
This life
Breathes
Truths
Yes, we do try to
Listen then
To these pronouncements
The Loving ones and the Blessing ones
But we are going nowhere my friendless friends

The needy
Christ
Have been hurt enough
While
Others cry
Didn't we
Cry enough?
And who can know this
In this planet
Of woes
Where sorrow
Is our religion?

Christ!
Saviour!
Guide us to hope!
Because
Honestly
We can see none
And we're losing all sight of you

It's hurting
Just to live:
Being abused
Being beaten
Being chained
Being poor
Being hopeless
Being spat at
Being mentally ill
Christ!
Just where exactly are you
In this bewildering wilderness
Wherein will we all reside?

Sweet ones
Trust in me
I did love you so
My sons and daughters
Not that it really matters
In the long run

෨෬

When Your Inner Mind Talks to You and You Don't Listen

Too many humans thinking!
And they 'think', they are thinking
That's what I'm seeing;
This man, that woman
Struggling to pay bills
Drinking liquor to forget senses
Why not?
You got something better to say?

6. Too many humans working ugly
Offensive jobs
Demeaning wages
Others are begging
For those demeaning jobs
As they lounge about
Doing
Well, doing
Nothing, in fact
Too many humans
Are being hurt again
Tonight
The existence of life
Hurts and pricks and pierces
You thought, 'Well, maybe,
Just maybe
Not tonight?'

7. Does the circle have a beginning?
You fools!
They spit at you
And then you exclaim to me
Incredulously
"Ayad, it's raining! There's Hope!"

8. People!
All six billion of you
Forget hope
Think
Of salvation as your
Exit
Or, if you didn't get that one
I mean: Death!

9. Your children will turn against you!
Friends are temporary alliances
That serves needs
And needs cease.
Your beloved 'friends' will cease
So turn your face
Turn your mind, turn away your eyeballs
To that which is facing you?
And that which overwhelms you;
There are people
Tonight
Enjoying their caviar yachts
And their sickening opulence
Need I describe anymore?
No I do not.
They're loving it
I mean, they're loving
Life
Because for them
All is gold, diamonds
And infinite amounts of money

10. So then, ponder, ye sad souls!
Sickly beasts
Slithering here
And struggling to breathe there
What is the distance between
You
And these posh monstrosities?

11. Think therefrom!
For my questions I pose to you
Have a purpose!
But I know full well
What you say to me
What kind of poet are you?
All you write is of negativity!

12. How correct you are, beasts of burden that we are!
You are right
Because that is all we are
Meant to be
Beasts of burden;
Till we suffocate from
Our exhaustion
And die.

13. You talk, converse, gossip
Do this work, build
Feel every emotion;
You create, destroy, paint,
Watch Television
And you
Listen to the news.

14. But did you ever listen to your own news?
No?
Well, do it
Listen, feel, experience your own news
And don't be shocked to hear of
Earthquakes in your own mind.
You feel sorrow for news of others
But watch your own tattered fabric
Of your mind and its remnants.

15. Listen!
Did you hear the news
Of the civil wars
Going on in your supposedly united mind?
Did you hear the news
Of the famines and starvations
Going on in your supposedly fulfilled soul?
Did you hear the news of the random murders that
Happened against your own unaware Self?
Did you hear the news of the rape
That occurred against your loving, trusting emotions?
Did you hear the news of the torture
That is being inflicted upon your isolated
Helpless Passion?

16. And, yes, I can go on, can't I?
All in all, you are going really nowhere
You are passive
Sometimes, you create initiatives of your own
But they are weightless
If I were to measure your entire weight

17. What?
You wish me to stop?
I'll stop
Read no more, then
And peace unto those
Who followed the correct path
Of love and dignity.

෨෬

Where Are You This June's Final Night, Baby Boy?

Hello Puppi baby boy
Where are you this June's final night?
I guess you're somewhere
And I'm here
Never near you
You're 5 and a half
And you say you 'love' me
But what do you and I understand by all that
My gerbil Puppi baby boy IZZET?
Whenever I pass by your empty room
I'm saddened
Whenever I see your baby clothes
Christ IZZET I'm saddened
But what can all that mean
To you or anyone?
What can it matter really?
Does it matter what I actually feel for you?
Pudu, Puppi, Christ I've made up a million nick names for you
Puppi PUZU
I love you simple
That's all there is in me
And what if it's too late?
Will it matter to you then?

ඊ

Where Do You Think You Are Going?

Who can think for myself
Thinking of you
Who lives to breathe
In that passion
I called your raging mind of passions
Seeking justice for all
Wasn't that accurate of me
In describing your holy self
Or was I wrong?
Yes, bitter I struggled on with whatever God left me with
That was what life dishes out to us all
You complain and for what purpose do you really think?
Dress what you want
Disguise yourself as much as you desire
You'll end up nowhere fool
You'll fly nowhere
Though, at moments, you'll feel like you were
Floating somewhere in some imagined sky
But all in all
You really were going nowhere.

☙❧

Where Will You End Up?

You live
You try
Living is
A confusing breeze
Herself uncertain
Someone
Knows
You're lying
Eating is easy
Being rich
Is simple
But you're unsure
Child
Uncertain night
Where will you end up?

&⁊&

Who Will Inform Me?

Upon a ladder
An angel decided to cry
Grief stricken emotions overflowing
Burned within treasures
Once desired
Fool's poetry mass-produced
In factories of slaves
Ignored by judges savants
Fool's poetry written
In a past still
Undefined
Sweetest moments
That wriggle out from within
Small child
Of a journey
Yet to end
Describing epic holocausts immense
While yawning listeners
Can never wonder enough
Yes, your trials
Are beyond us all
The verdict declared
Unjustly
Growing up
And separated for one decade
Till we
Are all allowed
To meet once more
Growing up
And who will recite
To me

When your face will burn
And who will inform me
Here
When you're bludgeoned beyond
Recognition?
Yes the kings
And their whores
Can do
As they wish
And banks gamble on
What can it matter
To anyone living, existing or dying?
Yes eternity
May resign
And challenges
May be ignored
In this particular existence
I inhabit within
In its space and in its time
Sins have been committed
But who will be crucified
For a hopeless cause
Tell me children
And wise ones?

⨀⨀

Who Will Save 'Humanity' From Itself?

Come down, and celebrate with us all
The beginning of a senseless
Murder
Where children sat awaiting
Trying to
Understand
The necessity
That you humans found in yourselves
Was so necessary to enact
Against the innocently impaled victim

I guess, that no one
Can ever
Accept truths
That for me and for you
Were so different
And yes, the medieval priest
Did laugh gutturally
In his drunken paradise

Yes, that man you loved
Was very sickening
In his punishing self-imposed bleeding dictums
And he can no longer talk
Through his burning tongue
That has been mercifully stabbed
Just far too
Many times..

Eternal laughter
That tries to memorize the renaissance poetry
Is a silly game
That gets you somewhere
Endless rows of frowning fools
I tell you
What did you learn from
All those poetry you did memorize?
I tell you
We must all decide
To stand
Somewhere of relevance and depths
Here in our personal hour

That God
Has dictated for us

Sing, then, the songs of deadness
Wherein the lonely dance
Hundreds and acres more
Of corpses have been recently
Unearthed
Rotting statues
And you can no more bear it
I know
Just as the world
Drowns her dulled eyes
Flying fast and far
Away from your memories

And now all the clowns disguised as priests
Have told me to die
So soon
I guess, they want me to say
"Goodnight"
But I will try to breathe
One more breath
One more escape
From this imprisonment
You classified as 'life'
You see, I wasn't really sure
If they weren't in truth
Priests disguised as clowns

Come tonight and throw your
Second-hand flowers
In that grave for
The princess that has been assassinated tonight
Murdered deeply
In this Paris night
And tomorrow we'll all laugh idiotically
In astonishment, once again
And the bewildered children will, once more, sit not understanding
The murderous nature of you human beings
And yes, I myself, once more
Do not understand what is impelling you all
To kill, murder and butcher again and again

Come ye saviours!
Save us, ye saviours!
The crucified darlings
Tearful you stand
I pray for you to rise up and do revenge
Against these sadistic monstrosities
In my increasingly disorientating brain
Christ!
I did try so hard to reach out to you
For you to save us
And my doubts are brimming now
As you wither ever more
Decomposing on that wooden cross

ॐ

Who Will Stand Meaningfully For Me?

From a world
Of suffering
Hunger and hurt
I stand
Sorrowful
In my mind that has
Nothing
Of significance
I reveal
For myself nothing
I stand
Standing
This life away
In a rage
Minutes crashing
Cursing me
Children laughing at me
Where even failure itself
Distances itself
Away from
Me
Communication eroding
But what can I do?
This is life
In its abnormal hurt
And terrifying twists
I scream
Within pointless dreams
Who then will stand firm
Meaningfully for me?

෴

Who's Afraid of the Madwoman?

A Madwoman who was once a juicy prize, now lies crumpled in that corner, named St.
Satan's Alley
Grinning in her furious stare at all her moments of void, though
She deemed them to be moments of glory indeed
And you stand there, glaring at this human's Epitaph that has already been erected for her
Dizzily Uncomprehending, severely questioning and painfully scared:
What is this? This is Madness True! My God! My God!
She screams out her irrational black vomit of words, sentences and ideas
Clawing, fiercely contorted, agonisingly twisted figure that is somehow 'human'
In abysmal resignation, shivering out such empty, empty Speeches and Sermons
Again and again: silly Mistakes after fatal Errors after horrific Failures
But, maybe her sermons weren't all that 'empty'?
Existing so pathetically, with such a demonic guttural voice
This is the Madwoman; yes, the selfsame flesh that looks demonic and angelic
How can that be? I am so confused, and dazed by this woman; this creature or beast
That was once the gentlest of beauties and the most inspiring graceful fawn
"Don't be frightened you fool – she's only a mad woman!" someone howls
Himself as severely mad as the Madwoman
The Madwoman, from what I can see, and from what I can understand
Lives in her flighty, flimsy world of euphoric fantasy and grim, bitter reality interconnected
In some antagonistic, feuding relationship
That at times deeply enthrals her
And at other times, deeply frightens her
Insecure and yet, selfish in the Architectures of her Mind
A pile of rubbish, wreckage and debris – she is now
Folly is her sadistic governor and an odd realistic embarrassing shame remains
Within her, flaring up from time to time
She can no longer understand human laws anymore
Can you understand this lass at all
Who can no longer understand the rules of life anymore
The rules that are written by you humans of course
Can you fathom her icy black wastes, plaguing her every twisted movement
And her every insecure, unsure, anxious thought?
Oh! She really is insane in her plateau of idiocy and unreason
Useless human being! No pity for you – I say!
Useless thing: no romanticism from myself to your ugly presence!
What winds sweep within you today and tomorrow – I do not care
Your failures, I can no longer care for
Go off and go on in your own demented paths of failures
I can no longer care.

∽∾

Who's Lying to Whom?

From my smile
I express
A horror
Of which
You all know
As we go on
In my life
That you explained
To me
As a faint lie
Just tell me
Then
Why I am
Why I am
Such a proof
Of all your lies?

ᔕᔕ

Why Care About a Mirage?

A mirage wept
Imagine!
A vision blurred
Its beauty disorganized
I saw death
I saw finality
I saw wailing monks despairing
I saw shaken animals weep for mankind's cruelties
I saw singers fake emotions of 'love' that they sang to wild enthusiasm from their audiences
I saw bland, hollow politicians be normal
I saw greasy doctors bored with the agonies of their patients
Here I am
We're all dispersed
Meaninglessly
We all talk by coincidence
We all love by coincidence
We all think by the laws of chance
And a mirage wept
Or, so I thought
It never mattered, you see
It never did matter
One way or the other

෨෬

Why Humans Are Repulsive

I think I like you
I really do
I think
You know
That I really like you
Woman!
Tear off that make-up
That weakens your beauty –
And now
Raise your eyes to be fierce, unequal that you are;
And do not ever be shy nor morbid -
This is your woman's life that God has unto thee granted
Be then what God wanted you to be!
Woman wholesome, fulsome,
Frothing with excessive feminine aches
Never be what you are not

Woman!
You, yes you, I look at you
I write to you
You who may read these letters
Embarrassment is another oddity
That - You - must shred off from your soul
Act sleazy act ditzy
Do what you wish, do what you need
But be always in charge of yourself
Woman!
And pander to whomsoever you think you need to
But only for yourself interests

The only truth, humans ask me
Is what?
Is what, you ask me, are you serious unto whom?
Are you laughing hysterically
At yourselves?
Who's disguising herself now again?
And who are you disguising yourself to?

Too many humans are lying
Too many of you are animals
I feel, I think, you are far too savage
To live in sanity's parishes,
Willowy heaths and yearning meadows

Christ! I keep hearing you screaming in my mind's blood
The same one that is critically sickened by this plodding planet
Wherein we all exist till our happy exit
You want to 'save me'? Really?
I do not want that 'Save' slogan for myself
I just want to Exit from here, Sir, Sire of the Lambs

"Who are you?"
"Where are you?"
"You do not seem to be normal, we really think"
Am I or am I not? I reply
Well, what did that ever matter?
"Wherefrom then do you write?" you ask me;
I write from lifeless lips, deadened words,
Departed heart, mired in frozen blood,
And flat fury
I write from expended ended energy, mania profound,
Bleeding black Rage
I write from the gutters of homelessness,
And nationlessness
I write from anger-grief, furious-rage,
Frenzied-hurt, boiling-abandonment,
I write from unfair bankruptcy,
I write from incurable mental illness severe
Yes I write because I am sick, you want me to say it again?
Sick! Sick for whom? For no one really
I'm sick so you can all feel so satisfied with your butcheries
Sledgehammers slicing, chopping human flesh
Frenzied butchering by humans against humans
Do you not see that which I see?

Give me another 'reason' to go on living, I think
I need to guess your pointless breaths
That scantily clad roam nowhere in my graveyard
That is meant to be for me
Evil humans, I've seen too much of you
And you've crucified me far too much in my brittle brain
Skinny skull, I hide from you, wife and everyone
Do not begin to 'talk' to me again
It is all just far too nauseous pour moi
Et tu veux un encore, et ca c'est contre moi
Tu ne sais pas ca?

☙❧

Why We Hate

As I sat there
My Shrill 'Worth' examining its unsatiated Self
And looking beyond at the flowing
And receding Crowds
Crowds abstract
Crowds of statistics
Crowds conversing seriously
I despised them all

Where did the tortured one cry?
Where do you finally displace him to?
Do you understand the nature of my question Man?
Do you feel anything in the flesh of your elemental entities?
Does your abundant flesh burn in the Fire of Truth?
Did you hate, as you forced us to play
In your life's circuses
Exactly as we so hated you?

Tell me transient humans
Where then are the last, lonely vagabonds?
Their worth well undocumented by your scribes
Humans are anonymous everywhere in this planet you imagined for us
To roam in only at your whims and will
Your spelling deliberately misdirected me;

Can we ever Scare the sorrows away
The sorrows you etched on our delicate bones?
I tell you
Tell your personality of the moment
To be fierce, unforgiving
Turn your desperation into hallowed odium
Where is hopelessness?
Turn its cold hands into detestation unimaginable
Gripping heartlessly
The oppressive nights must give way
To the highways of serene destinations unknown
And emotional depths will gather here within you
I tell you
Scour their fading bodies
Hating raging is lush in its vitalism breathing purity
To save the quiet hurt ones
What else did you expect from us, then?
From the perpetually downtrodden?
From the murdered ones?

෬෬

Will Boredom Cease?

Goodnight
Awakening comes
'Cross the lands, cities and rooms
So more repetitions persist
The continuation of talk that is made from chaos
And dialogue's empty exchanges
So much can be reasoned and felt
In moments
Where monotony replays its scenes all over again
And I do wonder at those souls who do wander endlessly
At this Theatre of Life
That we are forced into playing
For no reasons
Throughout our years
Discover not, I say, youth is being stolen
Nor beauty
But life
Your whole life itself is being stolen.

杨

Will Peace Ever Be?

Hooded oceans exposing naught of their mysterious smiles
Tempests are warning of uncertainties to plague us even more
The death of ages and eras is arriving
Your sorrows are kindling new untamed infernos
And the gentle, soft spoken candles of life are getting weary
Destitute, dispossessed souls
Their own burning tears they are forced to drink
Bitterness' sly and sarcastic droplets
Sadness is desperately grieving for your forlorn needs
Strange journey that is called 'life'
Certainty is denied for sure;
Winds are hesitating wildly
And once familiar dunes of sand are now swaying uncontrollably
Where then we will we reach simple serenity?

Will You Now Understand Me?

I am a thought, that
Is temporary
And Changing
However
I have changed
I used to be
Thru forces
I never knew
Something happier

Beautiful babies of mine
I longed for stability
In my troubled life
Did you not really know?
I was forced by god
To suffer
Mental
Terror
And I Find no
Other expression for it
Will you then
Understand?

&

Wisdom's Spirit is Trying to Speak to You

Wisdom's Sprit
In the skies of a melting evening
Human neglecting
What is
Imagined and real
Sweating shame and acting deaf.

Wisdom's Whispers, I hear, are returning
Suggesting, hinting to you, of
A landscape of desolate hurt
And passionately beautiful pastures and the freshest of meadows
'Cross the lands of lush flowers and thick woods.

Trembling hands, in fear from their insecure anxieties
And shattered glass has been created again by Man
Shocking the Guests of Civilization
While criticizing humans insist on criticizing
On dragging you
On the freezing streets paved with jagged deceitful words and masked feelings.
And the decrepit Mother
You knew of
Seems to have been
Molested
In her youth;
You never thought of that
Or cared for anything else much
Did you?

But the confused, irrational breezes
Interact
And may hurt you
So, typically, you turn away
Without listening,
You turn away into your fragmenting insides
And getting deeper within your Self of blackness
Forgetting this dreamy
And very real
Moment
Of Wisdom's Sprit
That is trying
To speak to you in vain.

∞

Woman Butchered

Child that gathered knowledge
Knowledge frightening to human nature
Girl-child was awakened
Herself she awakened
Saw the glow of eyes buttery
Glow of hatred molten
Glow of rape howling
Child, pretended innocence pretty
Child smiled all along the paths unknown
Yet, her body recognized colours unimaginable in their serenity sublime
Figures in her sleep strange, yet beautiful
Songs of sweet sleep, yet alerting in their soothing abilities
Little girl, who are you?
Why won't you let us
Define you?
Little girl
Honourable lady woman
Did you grow up at all?
Or did you just die in your infancy?
As so many before you have
Did you come
To feel and understand
Your sensitive dimensions?
We would have made sure that you would be mature
If you were submissive enough for us!
Child girl, laughs uneasily and seriously
Child girl, sees lofty, exalted visions possessive
Visions of history's episodes are expressed pointedly in your compulsive embraces
The foolish martyred are reading holy sermons for their self remembrance
Soldier unknown unmasking his face mangled to the surprised horror and utter disgust
Of his family, friends and other serious clowns
Singing an anthem of Fate's real truth and nature and essence
Heroine unnumbered, chained to deformity
And becoming a mirror of what they did chain you to
Child girl scarred and petrified by disturbed scenes committed lovingly and lavishly by
Man
Child girl curls, yet anticipates
Listen! The foot-steps frighten you once more
The shrieking manic clown has arrived again, red eyed and even more
Laughing dreary, spitting words jumbled and aloud
Figure of shame stands in front of you
Intents pre-arranged by his late father

Little girl!
Are you a woman yet?
Hearing swirls of delirious, sickening
Madness, uncontrollable panic and deathly angst
Hearing painter's brush strokes that scream their gasps of breathlessness out
Loudly and chaotically
Hears the anguish of colours' contrasts and contradict each other to the point of
Serious suicide
Little child! Sees the begging deaf pleading for choirs heavenly to sing seriously
Sees the miserable, emaciated crumbles crumbling,
Yet foolishly searching for a non-existent tenderness in darkness painted by drunken Satans
With the foulest, blackest oil colours in their leprous fingers
They try to paint you; define you
Analyze you; dissect you
Categorize you; classify you
Little girl; woman; virgin?
Alone and sincerely and deceptively guided by complicated, intertwining hatreds
That severely despised the existence of each other's truths and falsities
Feeling sovereignty abused by casual, bored
Unconcerned sub-humans in powerful positions on earth
Pierced in pain
My sweet girl, you are now
Pierced in deathly, unforgiving
Pains and hatreds never forgotten
Sweet Humanity
Sweet Man
Sweet human beings
How sweet you all truly are!

&c

Woman Prophet

The words I heard
The words herein preached:
"SNOWLFLAKES FOR THE HUNGRY
WHILE OTHERS CELEBRATE THE WEATHER!"
And little else, I understood
Prophet woman
Spreading leaflets
Speaking on soulful misery
Was gunned down
To a deathly cadaver
And the people walked on
In their lives routine
Yet, her words
I still hear
Though all else is gone
For now.

৬৩

Woman Speaking the Truth

Woman hungry
Spoke her Holy Text
She wrote it
In colours fractured and twisted
Spoke her words personal
In mists veiling her desires
And the desires of discarded Humanity
Here, self-proclaimed 'artists' gathered to conceive 'meanings'
Here philosophers and thinkers came to
Think and philosophize about the abstract nature
Of uncertain, unsure abstractions
In cafes and bars
Where politicians argued about the deniability of morality
And the beautiful nature of profits, at the expense of the sought after voters
Where prostitutes mocked the putrid hypocrisy of them all,
Here, in this crowded cafe
Where the lonely envied all
Where the eccentrics attempted to fascinate humans, but failed
With naught behind them

Hungry Woman!
Saw the sceneries daily
Nightly
Where the hours ran well past midnight
How many humans are hurting
This midnight
This mad hour
Turning to the waiters and waitresses
Who needed money?
Smiling in their weariness
The academic crowds carried on in severe earnest
Trying to precisely define uncertainties
Via mathematical certainties
The illustrious crowd was fanatically attempting to discover the exact
Nature of vagueness within the imprecision of life itself
This was, after all, their existential quests – do, or get drunk

Finally;
Woman Hungry
Screams her Sacred Words
Aloud
Words ringing aloud
"Where's Unity?" she shrieked in a searing voice

She finally
Echoed History's tears and
History's demands that Man
Finally be held responsible
For what He has done!
"Where's our sorrow?" she screamed!

"Where else can we be, but United?" she screamed!

The crowd paid zero heed
Crowd saw, heard and felt zero
Zero,
Save a
Deranged
Hungry Woman.

೦ಞ

Womanhood List

See the wandering woman
Made of Dust and Forgiveness
Seeking the bounty
We all read of,
By a room
Empty and alone
Frightened and freezing
Staring blankly
In a life
Of borrowed pride.

And the bride
Seeks Death
In her Union
Of lies and legends
Primitive and modern
As the children
Vanish in an adulthood
So soon
Where all is forgotten
Somehow
In emotional debris
Lurking in sorrow.

Woman of this life!
Your Womanhood
I cannot find
And so
I too
Must journey on...

৯৫

Words of a Prostitute Imprisoned for Being Insane

What do I think
Who I am?
I do not know
Who am I?
I am nothing.
That, I think, I know

My 'dignity', my 'morality'
Are scattered
As my meanings are
My entire being
My mind's entirety
Is scattered
To have any meaningful meaning
Do you like that?
I mean my words?
Do you like my words?
I lay down in my cell
And sometimes I entertain myself
Are you entertained?
Am I doing any good job for you?

I am and have been
Hated and loved
By idiots, all over and everywhere
And, anyway
They all receded from the muddied shores
Of my persistently timeless memories

I am a 'human'
I think
I exist
Because I have a few shaky
Facts to support me and my case
I Believe in nothing that claims to be eternal
Because everyone surrounding me
Are liars killers and simple-minded thinkers of murder
Exquisite
With a love for their needs that is surely equal to
Any
Fish
With its Cold brutality

Passionate blood bursting with heat
Evaporating
And then you'll need more heated
Blood
No?

I live in a box
You called apartments
Are you 'humans' serious?
Wages stingy
Prices posh
And how then are we supposed
To make our east end and our west end meet?

Man you bastard!
You have has only committed crime after crime!
I tell you screaming
You're the only animal
Who needs to blush
From your vomity lies
That you have been force feeding us
And they have been
Searingly etched all over
My skull, my dry brain that has been pounded by your lying fists
You who 'promise' me 'love' and 'happiness'
And then you all deceive me
Leaving me alone

Unknowing humans
Are you really so 'unknowing'?
I'm not sure, myself
Now when I look at you all
In the streets, in your homes
I feel, yes, that
You can't think
You can't feel
That is certain, for my security of truth
Your intelligence smells
Ape-like to my sensual gaze

Beauty
Can you ever succeeded
No no no no
Beauty is well beyond you
Yes, you are beautiful for this moment
But didn't you kind of notice
Your soul is cracked, my Dear

ෙ

Words of Advice From the Devil

Whenever a Devil speaks of Evil
Think, then, of Mankind
That chose and chooses still to love him
In a wilderness of hatreds that are so in conflict
Against each other
Killers can only dream in this land
That is so satisfying for them
For the countless repulsive, evil blind dwarves
Who travelled in their life
From port to port
Seeking more loving victims –
I say;
Accept realities
Accept truths
For sacred scriptures
Are being forgotten
By people
Of no significance
For the gods of governance.

❦

Words of the Raped Woman

In my instances
Where I can feel
The sceneries that change
And I don't notice
And the conversations that remain routine
I stick by the event
The hour that holds me
Where did I dance last night
I ask my children
This is my life
Disguised by my words

And I laugh too much
I must hide it all
Because you may think me mad
And we know the consequences of all that
Strange my laughter is
I don't know what I look like when I laugh

But I believe I look hideous, frightening
Because it is a frightened laugh really

But I never care too much
My evenings drag on
I eat what is being offered
I cook what is there
I watch what is being presented
I listen to what they feed me with
I judge too much
My fists are burning now
The number of times I have punched myself is embarrassing
The bars, the clubs, the restaurants, the cocktail parties, I can be seen there
All of them
If only your eyes were wide and deep enough
I am no mystery to anyone
I am there in front of you

I am the painting your imagination has created
I am the slab of flesh presented as bait for all of you
I am an attraction
I exist to be attacked by compliments
Compliments are the key to attacks
The first signs of the storm

A fresh human wave assault
And my fortifications weaken
Melting under society's suns
Yet, to eternity, I must hold out against the waves of deceit
Or I shall drown in death
Furniture stores
Don't they make you think
We too should be placed there

Far safer than the open cageless zoos of the city
In a furniture store it is far more calm and dignified
Priced objects we are
Married objects
Contract for life
Marrying someone is your life
Marriage is your death living
Marriage is your desperation for escape for security
And what a shock will curse you soon

People ask me about revenge
Revenge against whom?

Against everyone, everything and everybody really

Against television
Against schools and universities
Revenge against parents
Against museums and book shops and libraries
Revenge against philosophers and media people
Revenge, bloody revenge
Life has taken revenge against us
So it is against life and its contents that we must take revenge
Now that cannot be, can it?

O! My moments are not being lived out
I know, I feel my soul losing life
Between me here
And what can I do

That is the question

My life has sat down
The years prepare nothing for me
I exist to exist
I exist to work
I don't work to exist

And when there is no work
I exist, living between the minutes and hours

There is nothing out there
Humans are evil
For the most part
That should be my epitaph
My accusation
We are all trapped
Trapped in a ferocious cageless zoo where no one feeds you
So tell the smiling optimists and clowns to drown themselves
What they are talking about is a perverse heaven they have for themselves
And they are pretending that heaven is everyone's heaven
It isn't
Heaven is a private exclusive club
Tell all the optimistic intellectuals, artists and elites
To shoot themselves
Because they know nothing of what dust tastes like
They are comfortable
And the comfortable should not speak for the uncomfortable

And tell all the idiotic literature out there
The intensely irrelevant works of art
Tell them to get themselves shot now
What do they speak for?
Whom do they speak for?
Their art does not affect or touch us here in our pits of human degradation
Art is an irrelevance

Life is an irrelevance
All we hear is an irrelevance drowning us incessantly
Blaring out its dysfunctionality every second of our lives
Everywhere and every time
All I hear is the hollow mass-produced prefabricated talk
It is all Xeroxed endlessly
From one putrid mouth to another
Maggot infested mouth insisting on kissing your immaculate mouth
And we must listen now mustn't we
Because you'll otherwise label us as rude or paranoid

Humans are television sets
Living television sets
In the ugly flesh
Squirming and spouting the exact same vomit rendered glamorous by technicians
The same technicians who mass-produce weapons to deform, kill and torture
It is all the same really

Physical or mental
All the same
Maiming us
Driving us insane with a deformity well beyond our realization and grasp
A deformity you persist in calling humanity

You want to hear about my rapist, don't you?
That is the titillating part now, isn't it really?
I'll tell you all
I'll bare all
Because, like others, by baring all, I feel I am cleaning myself
Like old Pilate washing his sick hands
Well my rapists' name is Antssiranana
He was famous
He was a carpenter
He was glamorous
He was rich
He was a pizza maker
He was a student
He was a great lover
He had a great personality
He was beautiful
He was a genius
He was an astronaut
He was a disco personality
He was in every music video
He was the star of stars
He was my father

He was the centre of fame
He was optimism
He was the high life
He was exclusive
He was an alcoholic
He was illiterate
He was the woman batterer
A child molester
He was the businessman
He was the senator
He was a train driver
He is the present and eternal dream of everyone
He is the dream of everyone who is dreaming
He is what everyone wants to be
He was already in heaven
And he liked to dabble with little girls
Dabble with what they had not yet discovered
Dabble with what they had not yet understood
Dabble with what was their best kept secret
He was a secret everybody wanted to unravel

෧෨

Words on Man's Folly

I am begging
A truth to believe
In itself

Why, can you
Or can you not?

Silly girl
You who travelled a thousand distant miles
Seeking your back's comfort
So, now I tell you;
Sleep, yes
Is bliss
Just when you get there.
But sometimes
Getting there
Can
So happen to be
The hardest part
No?

Man always get entangled
Why?
I ask
Entangled ferociously viciously
Gnawing against each other
Fanciful dreams of serious
Destructive ideas
In your minds that I can only describe as
Being putrid
And yet
You keep insisting on fighting
In your own defecating ways
And then what
Exactly is my role here
For you?
To be your spokesman?
Of course not!

For I am here to guide you
Though I have found that your eyes
Have been for far too long raped
Beyond wisest Man's descriptions

Man – evil cretin!
Being beyond sanity's pale
Being of moronic stature
What repulsiveness is so fiercely endowed within you?
The ancient vomit filled chambers of your cancerous heart
Speak your words of expressionless rage and endless
Blandness that crucify the mentally
And the physically Insane

Dear me
What countries can there
Be who do not legislate against Man?
I am a Mind, or should I say, I have a Mind
How can I **have** a Mind
When I am that very Mind itself?
Bewildering absurdities, ironies, imprecisions
Indefinables
Forcing me to think a little bit here, I think
You think, you sink, and you repeat your days
Every day
We repeat every action, emotion, feelings
Every moment
Again and every second

Repetitions – boring me to nothingness
The sense of nothingness
When Being is imprecise truth
And Truth is imprecise Reality
But imprecise reality herself is so unsure of her own definitions
Then how can we mathematically compute all these
Proposed equations of the Human Mind, then?
This is becoming a swindlers' circus, do you agree?
I am getting angry, and I do not accept anyone
Attacking my sovereignty and my decency and my reputation
Therefore, I withdraw from you all
Even though I may discreetly miss you all
Man is now talking to you, questioning you
You must answer them
And how do you do that?
By being democratic?
How do you answer the multidinous
Questions of the ossified fools
Stupidities, bland TV programmes, vulgar food
Retarded conversations
Humiliating relationships
Dead marriages, dead human relation interactions
Sweetly called friendships
Dead cities, silent, drunks hear them
Vomiting
Rapists enjoying their nightly nights out
Wages sarcastically pitiful
Too many energies being pumped inwards

ভে

Yet You Must Go On

If I were to try to understand myself
Would I accept that I was a criminal?
And if I were to try to understand this, myself
Would I accept that I was an ignorant phoney?
And if I did not accept my realities,
What then would I say unto myself?
I am a journey, as any of you humans are too
Isn't that so?
Chaucer, Shakespeare, Milton
You were sad
You felt the burdens
Of your lives, didn't you?
Or, am I so wrong now in my estimations?
Do you understand what you are doing?
And if you don't understand what you are doing
Then *who's* in charge of yourself?
"I don't know", you tell me
Yet, on you must go
And go on.

☙❧

Young Lady's Verses

From a lonely
Moment
Hurt and ashamed
To come alone
In my own
Eyes
I have seen
The passions
Of boredom
And my needs
Weep

As truths
So collide
In within myself
And I just
So try to
Breathe
In my own life.

✥

Your Truths That Hated Each Other

Did you forget
Your Truths that hated
Each other?
Won't they
Ever
Try to begin to understand each other?

&c

You're Just Dividing Out the Empty Pieces

Speak in planned and arranged words
Consumed with your Comforting liquor
And endless soon to be forgotten conversations
Of no particular value
The hurt ones
Have decided
They are seriously planning now
To invade
London
Probably by
Tomorrow tonight
A time of insane anarchy
A time of killer's lust
Being promoted
By suave PR corporations
Robotic fanatics
And visionary mass murderers
The secular and the religious have decided to be united
Leaving no one satisfied
The endless wars
Between my border
And your boundary
Idiotic squabbles
Killing millions
And hunger tearing out
Lives of those others
Living in lands of plenty
While we speculate here
On the philosophical merits
Of fox hunting
Try to get real
Try to be real

Killers killing the suffering vain lambs
While charismatic prostitutes poisoning the lives
Of the young ones
Preaching the virtues of simple chastity
To a squeamish audience
You're going nowhere!
You're just dividing out
The empty pieces
Within your own selves
Heavenly hatreds
Multiplying
Rage
Burning anger
Going down
And nowhere
A passion
Of necessary explosions
That are just getting
Nowhere

லை

Death of Man

For many the turbulence of life are inexplicable and profoundly frustrating our faith in goodwill. What is the essence of personal meaning in a world where human relations are becoming increasingly fragile? What is the meaning of this world when only one in a thousand will succeed in his lifestyle? And what of the majority others left stranded by forces that apparently none can escape from? What is the meaning of this world where millions upon millions are forced to work in underpaid tiring jobs? While the extravagances of wealth are accepted, tolerated, applauded and esteemed, where does that leave the rest of humanity?

The twists of hypocrisy numb and stagger, while our changing moods react to this world of ours. We watch pontificating and condescending authorities speak of facts and visions bearing little relevance that are in any way significant to the average soul.

We listen to the oft-repeated clichés people employ as language has become script for so many a pre-recorded programme with little room given for free thought. Conversations of blandness, set-piece questions and answers and people 'exchange' ideas and thoughts on set pre-defined topics.

The turbulence of life are numerous and dense. The sad quality of human nature renders much of our need for meaning and fulfilment a useless quest. The chaotic nature of the human mind renders our hopes and desires resting on fragile ground. For dependence on humans to satisfy our needs is a risky adventure, precisely because most humans are themselves lost with no identities and suffering a severe sense of one's security.

In truth, we are alone. Alone as any planet, for though you may be part of a constellation of 'friends' and 'family', and though you may be part of a grand interconnected web of interests and lifestyles and motives, you are still, in essence, alone as any revolving planet is.

In this vast universe where the uncertainty principle dominates, you exist in isolation with no adequate means of knowing your security of your journey's path.

This truth, in turn, grinds down upon your hearts as we walk our daily lives here there. The heavy truth is that we are all alone and that the caring ones are fast decreasing in numbers. Our world is being divided between the cruel ones and the frightened ones, whilst the brave, heroic ones are dying out, and an increasingly lame society and an increasingly brainless culture, renders it more and more difficult to continue enacting out that heroic role.

The Age of Quantum is the Age of Uncertainty!

The destruction of the self due to its gradual erosion and fragmentation. United personalities are being hacked away by the effects of a profoundly idiotic 'culture'. These poisonous gazes that culture spits out creates a decoherent, paralyzed sense of meaning to our daily lives.

It is far more comfortable to exist numbly rather than to exist with a thinking mind, because the latter frightens us, given the ugly truths of our reality. For to reflect upon one's condition is to divulge the secrets of who we are all trying to repress and hide. The hidden secrets of our hearts that would awaken our eyes to the sordid spectacle of human nature afloat everywhere are not so easily to bear, even though the hidden secrets of our hearts we all can know of - if we desired to seek.

For in truth, the real vision of human nature is far too exceedingly ugly to behold!

Yet your persevering repression breeds chaos and greater fragility. Repression creates rage and an increasing sense of being lost in one's own life. All creatures, great and small, the rich and famous, the hungry ones and the beggars, the middle class workers and the destitute unemployed ones all share one common grief: the sense of a lack of personal fulfilment for one's vital existential needs.

So what is this life teaching us? What is this life conveying to our impressions? As the days pass by, the years and experiences being remembered, what calculations do you create and what results do you deduce therefrom?

The different sceneries you witness, the deep conversations you have had and the experiences you have been through, what essences do you infer therefrom? For in the final analysis, do we not all have a personal ideology for fine tuning our attitudes and lives in a positive and fulfilling direction?

And what of those afflicted with a terminal illness? What greater paradox can there be in life? How can we equate the authoritative, pontificating steadfast words of some, when for some others extinction is a near certainty and thus making their brief lives so utterly wretched?

Paradoxes of life!

The soldier killed at the dawn of war and the soldier killed in the final hour of the war. The prisoner of war who is summarily chained to an enforced loneliness and a casual sentence of frightful solitude and brutality for an unspecified time. What explanations do we offer ourselves when we try to understand the words and meanings of the puzzles of life?

The delicate nature of all souls in their routine lives saddens us. The quick discovery that life's offerings are bland and predictable.

The architecture of loneliness; the architecture of gloom; the architecture of mass-produced, cheap, drab houses surround our bewildered visions: these are our home towns; these are our cities – this is where our solitude comes from. The extremely ugly row of houses, the high-rise gray buildings, the dull corner shop, the bleak streets are common sceneries we all witness and experience hourly. This, then, is the architecture in which we are to live our entire lives?

Well, I say there can be no proper, decent and healthy living in these repugnant circumstances. We can only repress our emerging grief and our daily dying and our hourly saddened sighs – if we choose to tune to ourselves. The repeated ugliness of the towns and cities destroys joy, creativity and our remaining hopes.

The morally empty lives we live. The fundamentally directionless lives we live. This is indeed destitution for rich and poor alike, for this lifestyle we are living through creates a crassness within our minds.

This is the ongoing decline of 'culture' that I am speaking of, and this is the exact same decline that every ancient civilisation once underwent, leading to their ultimate extinction.

This is our age of the decline and the deadness of our souls.

And as we surrender our sense of the self and joy to the opium, mass produced high-tech rubbish, nonsensical 'culture', so too do we lose our own minds.

The murder of Man is now abstract and no longer necessarily bloody: for it doesn't really need to be bloody at all.

The destruction of the human race can and is being carried out far more efficiently by the greatest propaganda machine that has ever been created: the junk mass media culture of entertainment, hype, stupidities, fast services, bumper sticker intelligence, plasticity of tears and the deliberate ignoring of our noble feelings and emotions.

৩৫

Feelings on Panic Attacks

What did I go through?
And worse?
What am I going to go through?
Do you wish to know?
I have fear of heights
Put me in a shaky plane
Driven by an illiterate drunk
Mechanically faulty plane
And a human threatens me
"Jump out of the airplane!
Or else I'll blow your brains out!"
Does that give you an idea of my panic pain?
Of course not
Because until you feel that exact pain I'm feeling
You can never understand, nor feel
That pain
It's as simple as that

For you men
Imagine
Someone
Slicing your testicles off
Gently
For you women
Imagine
Someone
Slowly
Tearing & ripping out each
Of your fingernails
And stabbing your eyeballs
And then Tearing them out
Gently

Is that fair
For one human to live through?
Because that's what I've been through
I live wobbly existence
I breathe within palpitations
I talk to you through petrified eyes
I drive
And suddenly
A primitive primordial shower of fear
Rains down upon me

Splintering and searing at my mind, my existence
I need to stab myself
To kill 'my' fear
And yes
That's what it is all about;
Fear
A fear whose end
You cannot believe will come
A Fear
You cannot survive
You cannot go on living with that Fear
Because it is simply too fearsome
Your every mental entity cannot survive through this ordeal

And what can I do?
Nothing
Pretend to be normal
Because if people see you act crazy then everyone
Will be
Frightened of you
And so to the best of my waning
Abilities
I must 'act normal'
Despite the fact
That I feel that I am falling from
The top of the Eiffel Tower

୧୦

Repeated Lives

I'm not sure if I'm seeing myself right
Do *you* even know?
I live gasping this moment repeatedly
My will, my hope is thus lowered
And I'm so aware of this stench

ॐ